DISCUSSIONS IN SCIENCE

Promoting conceptual understanding in the middle school years

Tim Sprod

ACER Press

First published 2011
by ACER Press, an imprint of
Australian Council *for* Educational Research Ltd
19 Prospect Hill Road, Camberwell
Victoria, 3124, Australia

www.acerpress.com.au
sales@acer.edu.au

Author's note: Activity 9 has been revised by the Publisher in
consultation with Hannah Rachel Bell
Edited by Diane Brown
Cover and text design by ACER Project Publishing
Typeset by ACER Project Publishing
Printed in Australia by BPA Print Group

National Library of Australia Cataloguing-in-Publication data:

Author:	Sprod, Tim.
Title:	Discussions in science : promoting conceptual understanding in the middle school years / Tim Sprod.
ISBN:	9781742860343 (pbk.).
Notes:	Includes bibliographical references.
Subjects:	Science--Study and teaching
Dewey Number:	378.17

Foreword

The world of education slowly seems to be waking up to the power of dialogue in learning. In the world of work and politics people are rarely asked to solve problems by themselves, working alone. The boss will set up a working group, or a committee, or a team to either find out what happened or to propose a course of action. This is tacit recognition of the fact that 'two heads are better than one'. And yet in education, in what is supposed to be a preparation for a productive, enjoyable, and fulfilling life most of which will be social, we still concentrate on individual achievement, on working it out by yourself. Cooperation with others is even viewed with suspicion as cheating or as piggybacking on others' thinking. Of course one needs individual assessments at times but surely some of the most valuable skills we should be instilling into our youngsters are the ability to work together to solve problems, to be confident in contributing ideas, to listen to others with attention and respect, to provide cogent arguments for one's position or to be prepared to change one's mind with good grace, and collectively to build a better understanding than any individual could manage by themselves.

The development of high quality dialogue in the classroom is central to a number of programs designed to raise students' general levels of thinking, including Feuerstein's Instrumental Enrichment, the Let's Think materials (Cognitive Acceleration) and the approach on which the activities in this book are based, Philosophy for Children. P4C, as it is known colloquially, is now a well-established approach to introducing the art of thoughtful dialogue into classrooms. In other contexts it has been shown to have long-term positive effects on students' abilities to think, to argue constructively and to solve problems. The P4C approach fundamentally changes the dynamic of teaching and learning so that the student becomes more engaged, has a better sense of ownership, and develops his or her general thinking ability (intelligence if you like) to a higher degree than would be possible by traditional teacher-directed methods. Generating constructive argumentation in the classroom requires far more than a series of rules or tricks for developing good dialogue but this book provides thorough guidance to enable the teacher to develop the art of managing debate for her- or himself. The general method of arranging the classroom and stimulating high quality discussion between students, lightly mediated by the teacher, is clearly described in the Theory section.

What Tim Sprod has done in *Discussions in science* is to show how the P4C approach can be applied in a science context in the middle school years. Teachers of English, drama, and history are quite familiar with the process of engaging students in debate about issues such as character, motivation, and right and wrong, very often in situations where there is no one right answer. Science teachers (amongst whom I include myself) are less familiar with the art of managing students' discussion and yet, as this book shows, there are innumerable debateable issues in science involving such topics as different ways of interpreting evidence, ways of designing an investigation to yield a reliable answer, popular conceptions that what is 'natural' must be healthy and the very nature of science itself.

Each of the 18 activities in this book offers an opportunity for class dialogue that will expand students' minds, make them think more deeply about the nature of science and develop their ability to engage in debate about the applications of science in everyday life. Combined with other more traditional ways of teaching science, such as empirical investigations and teacher-led expositions of theory, the use of *Discussions in science* will provide students with a fully-rounded science curriculum. The activities can be used flexibly and may be introduced in any order as and when opportunities arise.

A final word: if this type of teaching is new to you, don't be put off if initially it doesn't work as well as you had hoped. Teaching for the development of thinking is not an easy option and it requires practice both by you the teacher, and by the students who have to become accustomed to a novel way of working. Persist. The rewards for you and for your students will be great.

Philip Adey

Emeritus Professor of Cognition, Science and Education

King's College London

To
Ann Margaret Sharp, d. July 1, 2010
Matthew Lipman, d. December 26, 2010
Gareth Matthews, d. April 17, 2011

Three giants within 10 months –
I hope my book is a fitting memorial to their huge impact.

Contents

Contents

About the author

Dr Tim Sprod has taught science and philosophy in Australia as well as Papua New Guinea, the Bahamas and the United Kingdom. With a first degree in geology and geophysics, he has also worked as a volcanologist in Rabaul, Papua New Guinea. While he has mostly taught secondary science and philosophy, he also has wide teaching experience across different subjects and age groups, ranging from early childhood to university.

He is Chair of the Association for Philosophy in Tasmanian Schools, past Chair of the Federation of Australasian Philosophy in Schools Associations, and past Secretary of the International Council of Philosophical Inquiry with Children. His books include *Books into ideas* (1993), *Places for thinking* (with Laurance Splitter) (1998) and *Philosophical discussion in moral education: The community of ethical inquiry* (2001).

For many years he has been vitally interested in effective discussion in the classroom, utilising the community of inquiry. His Masters from the University of Oxford investigates the efficacy of this methodology in science teaching, and his PhD focuses on the place of such discussion in moral education. He has travelled widely, and conducted many workshops in Australia, New Zealand, the UK, the USA, Singapore, Japan, Thailand, Iran and Hong Kong.

Preface

The aim

The history of science education can be presented in three phases:

Phase 1: 'eyes-and-ears-on science' – teacher centred lectures on scientific theories.
Phase 2: 'hands-on science' – student centred practical experiments.
Phase 3: 'minds-on science' – inquiry centred teaching for understanding and linking.

This book is concerned with how teachers can engage in the third phase.

Discussions in science is designed to help teachers in the middle years of schooling (11 to 14-year-olds) use classroom discussions to achieve minds-on science. While a rich science course will contain elements from all of the above phases, the third phase adds another layer by allowing students the space and opportunity to make sense of, and build meaning from, the first two phases.

The means

The core teaching method recommended in this book – discussions in a **community of inquiry** – arose from Philosophy for Children. These two concepts will be explained in more detail in the Introduction. In this book I will show you how running such discussions can help deepen your students' understanding of:

- key science concepts
- scientific thinking
- ways in which science works – what it can and can't do
- connections between what science students are covering in class and their everyday world.

Your role

This book relies on your professional judgement and experience in teaching science. The stories and activities provided are not meant to simply be followed. Rather, they are raw materials for you to adapt and incorporate in ways that will best enhance your teaching.

Your professional judgement is central – certainly in choosing which stories and activities to use and when to use them – but even more so in running the discussions that follow, as I will expand below.

More than that, your experience with facilitating such discussions will, in time, allow you and your students to enter into a community of inquiry from many other trigger experiences. These will include ones you deliberately design but also, most importantly, ones that arise from seizing the 'teachable moment'.

Acknowledgements

Not surprisingly, in a work that encourages and values collaboration, I must acknowledge the impact others have had on my thinking – far too many to name individually. I have used these stories with many science classes and workshopped them with many teachers and colleagues. Each time I have learned more – the fruits of which appear in many of the discussion guides. I thank them all.

I first started writing these stories as part of my Masters at the University of Oxford, under the supervision of Joan Solomon. To her I owe a huge debt, for her excellent feedback – and friendship – at our frequent supervision meetings. I also benefited from discussions with other staff and my fellow postgraduate students at Oxford.

For introducing me to Philosophy for Children, I will always be greatly indebted to Laurance Splitter. He has been a source of encouragement and wisdom to me for many years. There are many others in the Philosophy for Children world, to whom I owe gratitude for their influence on my work, but I would like to mention three by name.

Matthew Lipman's philosophical novels are clearly the models for my work, and both the community of inquiry and accompanying teachers' manuals were the brainchild of Matt and Ann Margaret Sharp. It was Ann who urged me to consider doing postgraduate work, and suggested I apply to Oxford. I also had the good fortune to work closely with Gareth Matthews on a number of occasions: his thoughts on children and philosophy have been an inspiration to me.

Finally, to Anna, Liam, Owen and Corin – my family – every time I discussed my work with you, it was enriched. Thank you for all your support.

Introduction

As one of the key drivers of modern society and prosperity, science is hard to ignore. Yet attitudes to science can be polarised. Many people, it seems, blame science for increasing environmental damage, for the obsession with technological gadgets and their accompanying greed, and for replacing a benign, natural world with a more synthetic and dangerous one. Many others claim that science is our only hope of salvation, saying that technological fixes based on 'good science' are the sole means open to us to solve our most pressing problems.

Attitudes of young people to science can become fixed early in their lives. Their exposure to science in schools plays an important role. Politicians and educational leaders have assumed that science education will lead to a populace that is better informed about, and more positive towards, science. The evidence is, however, that for too many students, the opposite seems to be true (Tytler 2007).

The increasing role of science in society, and especially the economy, has seen science take a more and more important place in the curriculum. This is a relatively recent phenomenon. Not much more than a century ago, the best education available had a heavy classical emphasis: science played very little or no role. As science education was initially introduced, it was highly theoretical, delivered largely through lectures and demonstrations. In the mid twentieth century, the idea that science education must contain a large practical element arose, and schools built science laboratories.

Towards the dawn of the twenty-first century, it became increasingly obvious that hands-on science is not enough: we need to have minds-on science as well to take science education beyond the learning of scientific facts and practical skills. Recent work by Jonathan Osborne et al. (2003), for example, calls for science education to embrace teaching students about the variety of scientific methods and testing; the use of creativity; the human nature of science activity; the role of questioning in science; the diversity of scientific thinking; why the analysis and interpretation of data may differ between scientists; the provisional nature of much contemporary science; the roles of hypotheses and predictions; and the importance of cooperation and collaboration in modern science.

One challenge at the heart of this move is the recognition that students do not automatically accept what they hear: they actively construct their scientific understanding and incorporate this understanding into their broader knowledge base. Without explicit attention from teachers, these constructions can be faulty, full of errors and misconceptions. There is a need therefore to make students' thinking visible to teachers, in an environment which allows critique and correction.

A second challenge has been a shift away from science education, preconceived as merely education for the technologically elite, towards the idea that all citizens in a democracy must be scientifically literate. The 3Rs of the traditional curriculum privileged English and Mathematics, but now Science is also seen as a core part of the curriculum. Courses such as Science, Technology and Society (Solomon 1993) and Science for all Americans (Rutherford & Ahlgren 1991) have been devised.

When combined with the trend towards mixed ability classes, the need to educate both future scientists and future citizens has made the delivery of science education considerably more complex.

A third challenge is that, as noted above, this greater emphasis on science in schools has not had the desired effect of raising the public standing of science. Too many students still leave school, distrustful of science. Many see it as disconnected from real life, too academic, even cold-blooded or intrinsically evil. Think of the common stereotype of the mad scientist, a figure that goes back at least as far as Mary Shelley's *Frankenstein* (first published in 1818) – an image which is explicitly evoked in describing all GM crops as 'Frankenfoods', whatever their merits.

Of course, the roots of such thinking are deep and varied, and school science cannot heal them all on its own. Nor do I mean to imply that science is entirely without problems. Just because science *can* do things does not imply it *ought* to do them. Scientific research and advances in technological applications need to be subjected to scrutiny, and only a scientifically literate public can do this properly. Students need to be able to take a critical attitude to science – not in the anti-science sense, but in the sense of having an appreciation of the strengths, limits and weaknesses of science.

Nor is it only students' critical faculties this book seeks to strengthen. Rather than seeing science as a cold, purely rational pursuit, discussions of the issues around science can help students to see the creative side, and to appreciate the role played by the emotions in science – both the positive impetus of curiosity and commitment, and in weighing up when emotional factors are reasonable and when they are not.

This book aims to develop students' understanding of scientific concepts, and some of the methods and principles that underpin scientific thinking and activities in all fields of science. It seeks to help students integrate their scientific understanding with other knowledge. The theory in Part 1 explores and explains these aims in more detail, should you be interested in pursuing them.

You will notice that in Part 2 – the practical part of the book – there is something of a bias towards what are sometimes called the 'hard' sciences – physics and chemistry. 'Hard' in this context means mathematical and precise, and is opposed to the 'soft' (definitely not the 'easy') sciences, where complexity often means mathematics may play a lesser role, and description a larger one. This is in part because I have observed that upper primary and lower secondary teachers can tend to avoid the hard sciences (possibly thinking they are hard in the sense that contrasts with easy), and hence less accessible to their students. One of my aims in this book is to show that discussions in a community of inquiry can make all the branches of science accessible to all students.

The teaching methodology: Community of inquiry

In pursuit of the aims mentioned above, this book recommends that you engage in a scientific community of inquiry in your classroom. In the sense advanced here, the phrase 'community of inquiry' denotes a productive pedagogy that arose in the Philosophy for Children movement – the brainchild of American philosopher and educator, Matthew Lipman (see Lipman et al. 1980).

In the late 1960s, Lipman came to believe that children should be provided with the means to develop and strengthen their thinking from early on in their schooling, and that philosophical discussions of a certain sort were a powerful way to achieve this. Thus the idea of a 'community of inquiry' was born: a collaborative investigation of open-ended ideas and concepts, triggered by stories that contained philosophical provocations.

Of course, a classroom can be a community of inquiry in several senses (Splitter & Sharp 1995). In its widest sense, it could denote a classroom in which all of those present are engaged in the pursuit of knowledge, and many approaches could be used – lectures, practical investigations, small group activities, individual projects and whole-class discussions. In the original Lipman sense – the one used in this book – we are talking of a specific style of class discussion, which is described in more detail in Part 1.

While philosophical inquiry still lies close to the heart of the notion of a community of inquiry, many educators have realised in subsequent years that it can be used in other specific subject areas. First, there is a philosophical underpinning to all academic disciplines including science. Second, for school students, questions of understanding and meaning are inherently open, even in subjects such as science, where the official answers to questions may seem to be closed. Third, questions of the relation of disciplines such as science to our everyday lives, and our ethical stances, are not part of the more precise core of science, and therefore need to be negotiated.

Generalist primary teachers will find that the community of inquiry is a powerful method for increasing student involvement, thinking and motivation in science – and in many areas of the curriculum. Approaching a part of your work through this method will make science more accessible, and contribute well to deepening your students' grasp of not just facts and practices, but also what science is. It will help them to integrate science with their learning across all subjects.

As a specialist secondary science teacher, you will find that adding the scientific community of inquiry to your repertoire will bridge the notorious gap between primary and secondary schooling. It will help diversify your teaching styles, engage your students actively in their learning, and enrich their experiences of science well beyond the mastering of canonical scientific facts and skills.

This book invites you to use the community of inquiry to assist your students to build a deeper, more nuanced and better picture of science, its place in their lives and its connection to the world we all live in.

The rationale for establishing a community of inquiry in your science classroom will be outlined here in more detail, with a focus on the following aims:

- To investigate the claims I made earlier about the benefits of a scientific community of inquiry more fully.
- To explore the theory behind the community of inquiry, showing how this theory can inform your implementation of such discussions in your classroom.

While it may not seem necessary to read the theory in Part 1 in order to use the activities and other materials in Part 2 – particularly if you are already familiar with Philosophy for Children and the community of inquiry – there could be some danger in taking this approach. A familiarity with the theory and practical guidelines that lie behind the materials may well enhance your ability to use them as they are intended, and to achieve the results I have claimed.

What are the benefits of a scientific community of inquiry?

Conceptual understanding

I will outline two related aspects of conceptual understanding. First, students may not have a formal grasp of the scientific meaning of the terms or concepts used. Second, they may connect these concepts to their other knowledge in incorrect ways (or fail to make the connections at all).

The first aspect of conceptual misunderstanding that can interfere with a student's scientific progress is a failure to have a correct grasp of the meanings of key scientific terms. While scientists are well known for inventing new terms, they also take common words and give them a specific scientific meaning. If students take these terms to have everyday meanings, they can be misled in subtle ways. Take the term *energy*, for example. In everyday speech, it makes sense to talk of a brisk walk, after sitting in a stuffy room, giving you energy. Such a statement would be scientific nonsense. Even terms new to students can be misconstrued in a similar manner. For students, discussing the specific meaning of common words when they are co-opted as scientific terms will help them to sort out such difficulties.

If we take the understanding of meaning to be the ability to connect a series of related terms to each other and to our wider knowledge, we are led to consider the second aspect. Much attention has been given recently to the fact that many people have misconceptions in scientific matters, and that these misconceptions are remarkably resistant to change (Driver & Oldham 1986). While the source of these misconceptions has been hotly debated, that is not our concern here.

How can we create the conditions under which our students will correct their misconceptions? First, students must be able to articulate their understanding, so that any misconceptions they have become visible. Standard tests conducted in schools do not always uncover them, as it seems that the ability to answer direct questions correctly may mask deeper misconceptions. This seems to be because rote learned surface answers, which are available to the student in test conditions, have not been internalised and incorporated into everyday knowledge.

Second, students need the opportunity to discuss scientific ideas in ways that connect those ideas to other knowledge, thereby exposing those understandings to potential counter examples. In the attempt to build consistent and coherent connections between all aspects of their experience, students can correct their misconceptions (Howe 1996). A community of inquiry is an ideal place to do this.

Scientific thinking

Thomas Huxley (1854) was probably correct when he said that science is 'nothing but trained and organised common sense' (p. 45), that is, there is no sharp distinction between scientific thinking and thinking in other contexts. Even if scientific thinking is somewhat different from everyday thinking, good science still requires good thinking.

There is considerable evidence that young people learn how to think better by taking part in discussions where good thinking is taking place (Bruner 1986; Forman & Cazden 1985; Vygotsky 1962). While initially, they may not be capable of thinking individually at the level of discussion, as long as they can follow and contribute, they will gradually internalise the thinking capabilities used.

For such a process to take place, good thinking has to be made publicly visible. In many classrooms – even in discussions – the best thinking is not public, but rather thinking that takes place in the teacher's head. Students merely see the products of this thinking. Properly run classroom discussions bring good thinking out into the open (Dillon 1994; Splitter & Sharp 1995). The *Cognitive Acceleration through Science Education* (CASE) project (Adey et al. 2001) is backed by research showing robust and lasting effects on students' scientific thinking are achievable through methods somewhat similar to what I am suggesting. My research shows that the community of inquiry can enhance students' scientific reasoning (Sprod 1994, 1997a, 1997b, 1998).

The nature of science

It is possible to learn science as a series of well-established facts and laws. Of course, any good science education should give students a solid store of the accepted scientific truths of the day. Few science courses these days teach *only* facts – experimental science, for example, gets considerable attention. Nevertheless, students can and do get the impression that these experiments prove facts, and that science can, in the end, be reduced to a list of facts and laws: a list that is all too often seen as boring.

I contend that students also need to have a more accurate understanding of what science can and cannot do: its methods, strengths and limitations. Most of our students will not end up working in science (though an increasing proportion will need to be equipped with some scientific skills and knowledge). But all of them will end up being citizens in a community. In this role, they will need to be able to weigh up the scientific claims made by scientists and other social commentators.

Voters cannot be expected to know all the facts and scientific laws surrounding such current issues as the extent to which humans are contributing to climate change, or whether there is evidence that a supernatural being has intervened in the process of evolution. Future issues may rest on evidence and theories yet to be advanced. So, while it is important that students leave school with an adequate knowledge of current scientific findings, they must also have a strong, inherent grasp of the nature of science.

Of course contemporary science courses address this need. Many texts have a section on *the* scientific method, which takes experiments in which variables can be tightly controlled as central to science (Lederman & Lederman 2004). Many areas of science where such methods are impractical, impossible or unethical are commonly ignored. Ecologists work in situations where the complexity of systems is such that experiments are either too difficult, or result in ignoring interactional effects. Meteorologists cannot re-run weather systems with changed variables, and must therefore rely on devising mathematical models, with their built-in uncertainties and assumptions, which must be tested to see if they can account for past evidence before being used to predict future consequences. Palaeontologists use techniques that more closely resemble historians than laboratory scientists, as the creatures and events they seek to understand lie in the deep past. Astrophysicists study events that are particularly significant and took place long ago. These events are also so far away that they leave no trace other than the radiation emitted.

Philosophy of science is the discipline that considers the nature of science. Though I am not advocating a thorough or systematic study of the philosophy of science, these do raise philosophical issues. If students discuss them as they arise – as they seem to be important or puzzling to them – they will gain a deeper grasp of the endeavour of science. They should then be able to evaluate competing claims made about scientific evidence and implications in their adult lives as citizens.

Science and everyday life

To talk of students as future citizens raises the question of how students integrate their science learning into their everyday lives. Indeed, the same question applies to the abovementioned issues I have identified: conceptual understanding, scientific thinking and the nature of science.

Compartmentalisation of learning is of course a problem that is not confined to science (Hennessy 1993). And yet if students do not integrate their school knowledge into daily events in their lives, their understanding remains weak and shallow.

Teacher directed lessons, and even student directed investigations, can reinforce such compartmentalisation. While the students' attention remains solely on the science in their lesson, they lack the opportunities to make the connections to their lives outside the classroom. Of course teachers can and do frequently try to make the connections for students, by introducing examples. Student directed courses can ask the students to develop their own questions, and to design investigations. Unfortunately, the complexity of the real world means that, in many cases, it is not easy to devise an experimental design that is both simple and effective.

The seemingly technical and objective stance of science can also obscure the fact that many scientific advances raise ethical issues, as is inevitable once science is put into its social setting. Many students have strong moral commitments, and they can cast science as the villain. Certainly, questions do arise about the role of science in creating social problems, but there are also problems that science can help solve. Questions such as whether science should pursue all knowledge, regardless of other considerations, and whether (and if so, how) applications of scientific advances should be regulated are important social questions, and we should assist students to think them through. Too often, though, they are seen as not being scientific questions, and therefore not to be addressed in science lessons. The danger here is that they never get addressed!

This book harnesses the power of narrative to help bridge the gap between pure science and students' lives. It can be argued that we use stories to structure our lives (Egan 1986). The stories in this book are designed to engage students in an inquiry which includes important scientific issues. While students are not likely to have the conversations depicted in these stories very often, they are nevertheless familiar. And they model the sort of inquiry that you will want to hold in your classroom. Hooks – problematic situations – within the stories provide an opening for students to initiate inquiry with their own questions. The inquiry then invites them to invoke their own anecdotes and experiences, and to listen to those of others, as they explore their own questions. Supported by the structure you provide, these classroom discussions can tie together disparate elements of a student's life.

How do I build a scientific community of inquiry?

In this section, I will briefly survey the theoretical concerns that support claims that the creation of a scientific community of inquiry in your classroom will positively impact your science teaching. Throughout, I will emphasise the practical implications of these claims. Theory of course is of no use unless it informs practice, and I will endeavour to show how these theories can assist you to adapt your own current practice.

Constructivism

Constructivism is basically a theory – based on observation and scientific study – about how people learn. This theory can take a number of different forms. Here, I will be discussing the idea that each of us constructs our own knowledge and understanding of the world, based on our experiences and reflections. As such, it is a description of how learning occurs. It emphasises that we each try to incorporate new information into our present ways of understanding the world, so we are active creators of our own knowledge. We do not merely take and absorb someone else's understanding, as this understanding is related and presented to us. (Both Osborne 1996 and Solomon 1994 critique it from the science education standpoint.)

Expressed like this, learning can be seen as an individual process. The influential Swiss psychologist, Jean Piaget, points out that there are two major ways we can adjust our understanding (see Donaldson 1978, for an excellent summary of Piaget's theory, and a critique). If the new experience fits neatly into our present understanding, then we just add it on. If there is cognitive dissonance – a clash between the new information and our present understanding – the new information can be rejected outright, or we can reconstruct our present understanding in such a way that the new information makes sense.

The practical implication of Piagetian thinking for teachers has been to diagnose the scientific misconceptions their students have, and to devise practical experiences that challenge these understandings, so as to provoke cognitive dissonance. However, without proper support, such challenges can lead to one of the first two responses outlined above (i.e. add it on, or reject outright), rather than the desired response (to reconstruct our present understanding), and even then such a reconstruction might be wrong.

Social constructivism

The individualistic Piagetian version of constructivism outlined above is powerful, but it leaves out an essential factor: we are social animals, and the vast majority of our learning takes place in social settings. Indeed, we can argue that the possibility of such individual learning is dependent on prior social learning (Vygotsky 1962).

We can illustrate this claim by considering the ways in which language is learned. Clearly all human beings are born capable of learning a language, but if they are not exposed to a particular language within a developmental window of opportunity, they do not, and subsequently cannot, learn a language. Arguably social exposure to language is vital.

So much of our learning, and even our ability to think with any complexity, is dependent on language, therefore it is not surprising to find that social exposure is vital across a wide range of situations. Of course, once the capabilities are established, then learning independently can take place, but social construction of knowledge continues.

The best known theorist of social construction is the Russian psychologist, Lev Vygotsky (1962). He claims that each of us, at any given moment in time, has a certain level of capacity: what we can do on our own. Beyond this lie the things that we cannot handle on our own, yet we can manage as part of a social group. This he calls our *zone of proximal development.* Beyond are those things we cannot understand, even with social assistance. (This assistance is now commonly called *scaffolding,* e.g., see Bruner 1986.) It is quite possible that no single member of the social group is able to handle the issue in question, yet jointly they can. It is not necessary (though obviously helpful) to have one group member who is already competent.

When the group achieves something that some of the members could not have achieved independently, those individuals start to internalise that knowledge or capability. Eventually, they don't need the group: they have learned.

The implications of this theory are that our students will learn best when:

- they are in their zone of proximal development
- they are interacting with others
- their group provides appropriate scaffolding.

The scientific community of inquiry seeks to create these conditions. The first condition is met by inviting students themselves to ask the questions that will form the agenda for discussion. The second condition requires that genuine discussion takes place. Finally, while all members of your class can at times provide scaffolding, you have the final responsibility as their teacher. Each of these points will be expanded below.

Running a scientific community of inquiry

I hope that you have bought this book because you are interested in running a scientific community of inquiry in your classroom. As intimated above, this is a particular form of whole-class discussion on matters of scientific interest. It has specific features, to be explained below, which enhance scientific conceptual understanding, improve scientific thinking, illuminate the nature of science, and enhance the linkage between students' science lessons and their everyday lives.

The community of inquiry, as a teaching technique, was initially developed to facilitate philosophical inquiry (Lipman et al. 1980; Splitter & Sharp 1995). This community has the following five features:

1. Students sit in a circle or some other arrangement that allows them to see each other.

2. The story is read communally around the group, each student reading a paragraph unless they opt to miss out by saying 'Pass.'

3. Students are invited to share their questions about the story.

4. One of the questions is selected.

5. The discussion begins; the teacher's role in building the discussion is crucial, and is outlined in more detail below.

The above listed features could be called the 'standard model'. Like all classroom techniques, they can be modified to fit the context of the lesson, or to take advantage of the abilities and interests of the students. Such modification is a matter for the teacher's professional judgement. Nevertheless, each of the features has a rationale, and a teacher who modifies or bypasses any feature should be aware of the possible downside of that modification.

As we know, teaching is a highly skilled profession. You make many professional judgements in your planning before every lesson and, especially, during the lesson. Each decision you make leads the class in a particular direction: it opens one door and closes others. The open door will have certain advantages and possibly disadvantages but this also applies to the doors you decide to close. While there can be situations where there is one right door to open, often each door has pluses and minuses. Being aware of what might be gained or lost in altering the features of the community of inquiry will be important if you decide to modify it.

Preparing the ground

Circle

It can be difficult or time consuming to rearrange furniture in a room (so that all students can see each other) in a circle or similar set up. However, the message sent to students by such an arrangement – that they can talk directly to each other, and that such talk is valued – is important in establishing a discussion that is not always directed through the teacher.

Joint reading

To create a shared focus on the material, the story is read communally. Each student will need access to a copy of the story. (The individual stories are available for printing out or viewing online at <http://www.acer.edu.au/discussions-in-science>). Some students are reluctant to read in front of their peers, so an option to pass is necessary. Many students enjoy reading to the class. In order to avoid a string of passes, it can be useful to ask for a volunteer to read first. However, it is usually fine to ask each student to take their turn. In my experience, on the odd occasion (usually when I was trying to set up a community of inquiry) when some students exert pressure on others to all pass, then I merely indicate that I am happy to read the whole story. Having made some sort of point (and seeing I don't rise to the bait), there is usually no trouble with the joint reading next time.

Student questions

For me, asking the students to identify what they find interesting or puzzling in a story, and then putting it in the form of a question, is at the heart of the power of the community of inquiry. Thus the students set the agenda for the discussion to follow. This is how we ensure that the discussion lies in the students' zone of proximal development.

The process by which the questions are generated can be varied. The standard way is to ask students to think about what puzzled or engaged them, and to tell you what they come up with. The questions can then be written on the board, usually with the name of the student who asked it, so they own their question. It is important to gather all the questions before discussion, rather than jump straight into discussion, responding to the first question offered. Later questions sometimes build on earlier ones, and the most powerful question, or the one that interests most students, may well not be the first question.

In a group that has trouble asking questions, or who tend to ask shallow questions, it can be useful to use a 'think, share, square, share' strategy. Ask each student to frame their own question, then to share it with their neighbour. From this pair, they have to decide on one question to take forward, which may be one of the original questions, or a modified one or even an entirely new one. Repeat the process by combining pairs to make squares. Finally, collect the question from each square. This technique is also useful when a class starts to ask large numbers of questions. Of course, there are other collaborative-learning –based techniques which can be adapted to gathering these questions.

As you use the community of inquiry more often, you will generally find that the quality of questions improves, as students get a feel for the sort of questions that lead to more satisfying discussions. In the Philosophy for Children literature, such questions are usually characterised as open inquiry questions: they do not have an agreed answer that can be sourced, but the issue and its possible solutions can be clarified through discussion (Cam 2006). Certainly, these sorts of questions will arise from the stories in this book: they are often questions from philosophy of science.

However, the stories will also raise questions which are technically closed (in science, you can source many of the answers, or at the very least, the presently accepted answers, in a book), but which are effectively open for school students. An example of such a question might be: 'What does "energy" mean?' (see Activity 7: Energy). There is a clear scientific definition and there are less clear, everyday usages. Yet, if students are not clear about the difference, then an exploration of the possibilities can help them to clarify the issue much more than quoting the scientific definition.

Since scientific questions can be much less open than philosophical ones, a teacher leading a scientific community of inquiry will have to make some decisions about the extent to which they can lead the discussion towards particular conclusions, which would not be appropriate in a philosophical question. I'll discuss this issue in due course.

Selecting the initial question

There are several ways in which the initial question for discussion can be chosen. Perhaps the most common way is to ask the students to vote for the one they think would be the most (scientifically) interesting question. Sometimes one of the questions will create such a stir when it is asked that it is obviously the one to go with!

Other techniques include first asking if there are any obvious ways in which the questions can be grouped. If one issue collects a large number of questions, then confine your attention to that group, and identify which question seems to offer the best way to start exploring and discussing the issue.

Alternatively, especially in the early stages of the community of inquiry in your class, you might try to sharpen your students' grasp of what makes a good question for inquiry by asking them to identify questions to which there is an easy answer, or which are impossible to answer. The former include closed factual questions, where a little library research or a closer reading of the story will give the answer. The latter include questions inviting speculation about matters of fact, where we can never find the answer (e.g., questions about the motivation of characters in the story). The remaining questions will generally be the most promising ones for discussion.

It can happen, however, that your students will want to discuss the question that you see as the most unpromising. This is okay because if the discussion really doesn't lead anywhere, this will soon become apparent, and you can then move to a different question. Sometimes, though, even the most unpromising question can lead to rich and intriguing discussions, so it pays to have an open mind.

The discussion

The reading of the story and gathering of questions is merely a lead in to the discussion – the centrepiece of the community of inquiry. The aim is to create a meaningful, focused and rigorous conversation which shares the features of a natural inquiry: participants listen carefully to each other, respond to what they are saying, take turns and pursue greater understanding. If we can create a natural conversational dynamic, the joint construction of ideas that ensues leads to more cohesive shared knowledge within the group.

In the discussion, your role is not primarily that of supplying knowledge for students to imbibe (though this will sometimes be necessary), but of providing the model of an experienced thinker to the apprentice thinkers in the class to ensure the highest level of thinking is maintained. Since your students have set the agenda for discussions by asking questions that appeal to them, we already know that what is discussed is relevant and appropriate to their needs and abilities.

Before outlining the features of a community of inquiry discussion, it is worth contrasting this discussion with a common pattern of interaction in the classroom. There is much research to show that teachers who say they are having a classroom discussion ask closed questions, field an answer from a student, evaluate that answer and then ask another question (Dillon 1994; Sinclair & Coulthard 1975). While this technique can be useful, for example, in testing how well students scan recall content, it is different from the pattern of interaction that a community of inquiry seeks to establish.

We want students to drive the conversation, creating the time for them to explore ideas at their own pace. We seek a pattern where students respond to other students, with you as teacher becoming just another participant in the discussion. Of course, such a pattern takes time to build up, especially as students are used to looking to you for their cues. Further, you may appear to students to be taking a back seat as teacher, but the ultimate responsibility for maintaining a rigorous and focused discussion nevertheless remains with you, no matter how much students may take on some of this work.

Prior teacher preparation

As discussion leader, you must have previously considered the possible lines of development of discussion arising from various hooks in the story, even though you cannot be sure that any particular line will be picked up by students' questions. Of course, as you will be in a science class, scientific ideas are likely to be among those that are picked up, and you also have some control through the contributions you make to the discussion.

Prior preparation will assist you to identify the potential of remarks that students make, and suggest the right intercessions to make to help develop them. Each story in this book is accompanied by such discussion guides, but be wary, however. Finding the right balance between being over-directive (and thus killing genuine student inquiry) and too lax (and thus losing any rigour in the discussion) is not always easy, and will come with experience. As the agenda is set by the students and the actual direction of the discussion ought to arise from their enthusiasm, there is still considerable need to 'think on your feet', especially if they choose to go with a question for which there is no discussion guide.

Running the community of inquiry

Here are some pointers as to how to manage the community of inquiry:

1 Your role is that of facilitator. Basically, you will provoke and model the moves made by experienced thinkers in their own best thinking. Try to avoid the common teacher roles as a source of knowledge and instant evaluator of student responses: the community should eventually take on these roles. Some major techniques you can use are as follows:

- Try to increase your wait times. When you finish your own comment or question, wait longer before you rephrase what you said. When a student finishes speaking, wait before you respond. Research shows that teachers usually wait less than a second in these situations, but that increasing the wait time to at least three seconds has numerous, positive benefits, including greater length and quality of responses, more contributors entering the discussion and an increase in the intellectual depth of answers (Rowe 1972).

- Avoid making too many evaluative comments. Students learn to use such comments as rewards, seeking a 'good' from the teacher, rather than seeing their comment as just one part of a developing inquiry.

- Exhibit your own puzzlement. While you are obviously the teacher because you have greater knowledge than the students, and have a responsibility to ensure students increase their knowledge, many of the questions these stories raise have puzzled many people for a long time. If they puzzle you too, be transparent. Inquiry begins in puzzlement, and you can hardly expect students to inquire if they think you know the answer, but you are hiding it. The other side of the coin is that you should be wary of pretending you don't know the answer when you do. Be upfront if you are holding back because you are teaching them how to seek such answers.

- Use judicious questions and comments to signal cognitive moves that students might usefully make next. Such scaffolding of their thinking is central to the community of inquiry, so I will explore the sorts of moves that can be made below.

- Concentrate students' attention on metacognition. This can be done in two ways. First, you can incidentally label the sort of thinking that a student has just used ("Does anybody want to add to that distinction?"). This helps students to build up a vocabulary of thinking. Second, you can turn the discussion explicitly to the cognitive moves just used ("What makes a reason a good reason?"). The inquiry is thus taking its own tools as its content, and students are considering how to think better. Since their thinking is being done within a rich context, with students repeatedly applying thinking techniques to diverse contexts (as is judged appropriate by the participants), the likelihood they will transfer their improved thinking skills to other settings is enhanced.

2 Rules for the discussion can be decided by the community, either in advance or after some experience. Maybe your class already has such a set of rules, though discussing whether these rules need any modification, or addition, for the purposes of the community of inquiry can be fruitful. Students tend to heed rules better if they feel they have had some say in framing them.

3 The impact of the physical setting of a circle on the establishment of a community is reinforced by the encouragement of participants to talk to the whole circle, or directly to the person they are answering, rather than always through the teacher. While it can be necessary, especially with a newly established group, to insist on hands being raised before speaking, it should certainly be your aim to develop skills in turn taking, so that the discussion follows a more normal conversation dynamic. Deciding how far you will allow a noisy interchange to continue before insisting on one speaker at a time will be one of your major judgements.

4 You are a member of the community and thus have a duty to participate in the discussion. However, traditional roles of teachers mean that any input you make will carry greater weight than the contributions of students. Hence it is important for you to hold back in matters of fact and opinion, especially if there is a good chance that students may come up with an acceptable answer with suitable encouragement. Of course, there will be times when your input is just what the discussion needs; deciding when and how to do this forms part of your professional judgement, guided by knowledge of the group and your prior consideration of the issues involved. For example, if the class consensus seems to be arriving at an answer which is clearly scientifically inaccurate, you will probably need to step in. Your intervention, however, may not always need to be in the form of a dogmatic statement. It could be a provocation, requiring the students to rethink, or a suggestion that some research is needed, or a move to experimental work to check the validity of the conclusion.

5 You need to encourage recognition in the community that many questions are complex and not amenable to simple, quick answers, so enough time has to be provided for talking around problems and concepts. Clarification of the problem must be recognised as valuable, even if no answer is found. Premature closure of questions and discussion should be avoided.

6 Students must be encouraged to take responsibility for their comments and be prepared to defend, modify or change them, as and when appropriate. You need to seek to ensure that attacks on positions are not made or seen as attacks on the holders of these positions.

Prompting good thinking

One of the major aims of the scientific community of inquiry is to enhance students' scientific thinking. As facilitator of the community, you will be looking for opportunities to prompt students to deepen their thinking, and to make the right sort of cognitive moves to enhance inquiry. Sometimes, you will be modelling that thinking, in which case you have to remember to think out loud. Making thinking visible to students is a major aim of the community of inquiry.

Your contribution to the discussion could therefore be a question that cues a student to expand or extend their comment, or invite other students to build on the question in a certain way. It could also be a statement that labels the move the student has just made, or points to another move. You can be making the move, explicitly. Examples of each of these scenarios are given in the list below.

Attempts to provide lists of capabilities involved in higher order thinking have generally resulted in complex classifications that differ from author to author (e.g., Ennis 1987). So what follows is not meant to be a definitive list, but rather a checklist to remind you of the sorts of interventions you can make to sharpen the inquiry. Just when each intervention should be made is, of course, a matter for your own professional judgement. As you would expect your students to become more able to find an appropriate move to make in their thinking over time, you will also improve your ability to find a useful prompt at the appropriate time.

A good carpenter is not just someone who knows how to hammer a nail, or to make a proper timber joint. It is also necessary to be able to discern the right context in which to choose a nail, rather than a timber joint. Similarly, good thinking is highly contextual. This is why it is not just enough to learn the sorts of moves a good thinker makes: it is also vital to practice choosing and using these skills appropriately in genuine inquiry. You can help students by scaffolding that choice.

- **Identifying puzzles and questions:**
  Is there anything that puzzles you here?

- **Rephrasing and restating/clarifying:**
  You seem to be saying that …

- **Giving reasons:**
  Why?

- **Identifying points of agreement/similarity/consistency:**
  I think that you are agreeing with Sarah here.

- **Identifying points of conflict/difference/inconsistency:**
  Would that fit with what Maeve said?

- **Finding examples:**
  So, an example of that would be …

- **Finding counter examples:**
  Would that always work? Can anyone think of an example where it wouldn't?

- **Generalising/advancing rules:**
  So it looks like we could find a rule to cover all those examples.

- **Finding assumptions:**
  It seems to me that you are assuming that it would be easy to measure that.

- **Recognising implications:**
  Let's see what would happen if that were true.

- **Identifying relevance:**
  So how does that help us?

- **Identifying possibilities:**
  Perhaps there might be an alternative here.

- **Speculating:**
  What if …?

- **Drawing together ideas:**
  Perhaps we could sum up here.

- **Identifying progress:**
  Which of these questions do you think we have answered?
  Perhaps this is more complicated than we first thought.

You will be able to recognise that your scientific community of inquiry is maturing when two things happen. First, you should find that you need to prompt moves less often. For example, you will no longer need to ask what a student's reasons are for a particular assertion, because they will automatically add the reasons to what they are claiming. Second, you will begin to find that other students will do the prompting – or fill in the next move – for you. This is evidence that students are internalising the cognitive moves that you as teacher previously had to cue.

Ideally, you would no longer have to be monitoring the conversation for opportunities to provoke deeper thinking, as the class would jointly be doing this for you. In reality, as the community matures, you may well find more frequent and longer periods where this happens. Nevertheless, the final responsibility for maintaining a deep and rigorous discussion will remain with you.

If you are interested in learning more about the community of inquiry and how to run one successfully, I highly recommend Laurance Splitter and Ann Sharp's *Teaching for better thinking* (1995), and Phil Cam's *Thinking together: Philosophical inquiry for the classroom* (1995) and *Twenty thinking tools: Collaborative inquiry for the classroom* (2006).

Fitting the community of inquiry to your classroom

In the sense outlined above, the scientific community of inquiry is a specific teaching technique, to be used in conjunction with many other tools at your disposal. From these tools, you as teacher will choose the ones you feel most appropriate to achieve the aims which you have set for your lesson. Overall, your goal will be to create the best possible learning environment for your students.

It would be nonsense to claim that the scientific community of inquiry should be the only method you use in your classroom. It needs to be judiciously incorporated with the mix of lecturing, group activities, practical experiments, individual research and other methods.

Nor am I claiming there is a universal style of classroom teaching that is the best: teaching and learning are complex activities, always involving a unique mix of individuals. It would be surprising indeed if there were one absolute, objective way to teach that is always the best for all teachers in all classes. As a skilled professional, you have the expertise to find the ways that best suit the temperaments and styles of yourself and the class.

Nevertheless, I will claim that any classroom should loosely become a community of inquiry, that is, a community that is focused on inquiring after truth, meaning and understanding. In this sense, it seems to me, the more narrowly defined community of inquiry can be seen as a central methodology, which brings coherence to the broader aims of the classroom. This inquiry draws together all the other learning going on in the class. It gives you the best insight into the grasp students have on the work you are covering.

If the community of inquiry is working well in your classroom, then it will not remain a sealed-off activity. It will spill over into the other techniques you use. You will lecture differently, and students will respond to those lectures differently. In my experience, students will, from time to time, want to constitute a short and informal community of inquiry in the middle of, say, an experimental session. Such sessions, which may only last a few minutes, will not involve a story, or the gathering of questions, but arise spontaneously from a student's question.

I trust that you will find your scientific community of inquiry invigorating and exciting. You may well find what other teachers have found: students commonly express their delight in being able to share their own thinking, and to discover what their classmates are thinking.

PART 2
PRACTICE

This part contains 18 stories, together with teachers' notes and suggested activities. Each of the stories are available for printing out or viewing online in a classroom context at <http://www.acer.edu.au/discussions-in-science>. For more detail on how to use these stories in a scientific community of inquiry, please read the theoretical background in Part 1. Here, I offer some brief notes that assume you are already reasonably familiar with running a community of inquiry.

Activities

Some of the stories are accompanied by suggestions for activities to precede or follow the discussion. It is up to you to decide whether and when to use them. You may find that you want to modify them, or replace them with activities of your own. Obviously, how you decide to incorporate the stories is a matter for your professional judgement.

Science outlines

Many of the stories are accompanied by a brief outline of the science involved in the story, and the background ideas on the nature of science. How much you need to refer to this outline and background ideas will depend on your own science background. The book is aimed at the middle schooling years: a range that in many places crosses the primary/secondary school divide. Teachers vary widely in their scientific training: you may have dropped science as early as you could; or you could have a science degree. I have aimed to pitch these notes at a level accessible to all teachers. If you are a science specialist, you may find that you do not need to read all these notes in detail.

Discussion guides

Each story is followed by one or more discussion guides on leading ideas in the story. You will notice that the structure of these guides is generally the same: after the outline, they present a series of questions from the stories, which lead to more general, abstract questions concerning major issues seeded in the stories.

These discussion guides are not meant to be used as a list of questions to ask in a defined, formulaic manner (though you may occasionally find this to be a useful way to proceed). Primarily, their purpose is to alert you to the numerous ways in which you can move the discussion from the particular to the general. I suggest that you read these discussion guides in advance of the session in which you will use the story, and then draw on them as and when necessary to guide more in-depth discussion.

You may find that you don't need to use all the questions in the discussion guides, as the students will take some of the steps themselves. Or you may find the discussion moving in a different, but still relevant and useful, direction. In that case, you might choose to go with the flow. At first, it might be useful to have the guide in front of you. Later, I would hope you internalise the guides somewhat, and no longer need to refer to them. Sometimes the guide for one story may assist you with a question asked in relation to another story.

I have limited these guides to the science-related ideas in the story. However, the nature of narratives can raise puzzles or questions of many types – not merely those concerning science. How you deal with these non-scientific questions is up to you. You may prefer to let the discussion follow them, and use your own understanding to guide them. Or you may prefer to shift the focus to science-related questions that students ask.

Of course, the context in which the story is read will have an effect on the questions asked. If you are a secondary teacher, the context is quite clear: this is a science lesson, and therefore students will be predisposed to ask science-related questions. In a primary classroom, you may need to think in advance about how you create the context for the story. If you make it clear that you are moving into a science session, you may well find that students will be happier to concentrate on science issues.

Activity 1 | Magic

Prior activity

You could introduce this story with a little magic trick of your own (see <http:// www.illusioneering.org>). Perhaps you already know how to do one. Or perhaps you would like to use the following idea. This picks up on the trick Wai Ling refers to in the magic story: changing the colour of paint.

To make red cabbage water, finely chop some red cabbage and boil it until the cabbage has gone pale, and the water is a deep purple colour. Red cabbage water is a natural pH indicator – it changes colour depending on whether the solution is acid or alkaline.

Prepare three containers (small bottles, test tubes or similar) in advance as follows. Put a few millilitres of diluted white vinegar (acetic acid) in the first container. Mix a teaspoon of bicarbonate of soda (sodium bicarbonate) with enough water to dissolve all the powder and then put a few millilitres of the solution in the second container. In the third container, have a few millilitres of water. The three containers should look very similar to the class. If you can find containers that mask the presence of the liquids, the effect may well be even greater, provided no-one recognises that you have liquid in the containers. However, even if the students realise there is something in each of the containers, it will still be a topic for discussion.

Put on a bit of a magic act: make some magic passes with your hands, say a few magic words. Then pour some of the red cabbage water into each of the containers. The vinegar solution will turn reddish pink, the bicarbonate solution will go green and the water will remain purple.

For a more impressive display, you could do a little more prior research. The colour that red cabbage water becomes depends on the pH of the liquid to which it is added. So, you can get an impressive array of colours by priming your containers with a number of different acids and alkalis. Experiment with other substances. If you have access to a science lab in your school, you should be able to get several different acids and alkalis. Many ordinary household substances are also acidic or alkaline.

Wai Ling was really excited when she arrived at school on Friday – she ran straight up to her friends. Although Maeve was already telling them about her hockey game last night, Wai Ling burst out with "Where do you think I was last night? Mum took me out for a surprise and we went to this magic show! It was great! This guy could do all sorts of amazing things!"

"Like what?" Sarah demanded.

"Like turning purple paint into all sorts of other colours," exclaimed Wai Ling. "Like pulling rabbits out of a hat, and pigeons, and coloured scarfs. Like getting an egg from behind my ear and breaking some guy's watch, and then finding it all fixed in the handbag of some woman who was sitting rows and rows away. Like …"

"Like breaking into somebody else's conversation," muttered Maeve, who was about to tell everyone about the brilliant goal she had scored. She was more than a little put out.

"Oh, Maeve, I'm sorry," moaned Wai Ling. "I was just so excited I forgot my manners! But it was excellent, this magic show, it was …" She broke off in confusion. "What were you talking about, anyway?"

"I was talking about the hockey last night. I scored this brilliant goal. I was right in the corner of the circle and the goalie saw Jenny coming down the middle – she thought I was going to pass to her, so she came out to intercept it and I saw the goal just open – though not much of it from there – and I just whacked it straight in! It was magic!"

"That wasn't magic," said Wai Ling, "just luck, I mean tremendous skill." She modified her reply, seeing Maeve begin to scowl again. "Not *real* magic, anyway, like I saw last night. I mean, he just couldn't have done these things without using magic – they just weren't possible. But we all know how great you are at scoring goals."

"Well, yeah," conceded Maeve, a little mollified by the compliment, "but it wasn't magic at your show either, I bet. It was just trickery."

$\longrightarrow$

> "That's right," chimed in Sarah. "I bet he just got you to look the other way or something. There's got to be an explanation for everything he did."
>
> "Yeah, and the explanation is magic," said Wai Ling. "You weren't there – I was! I watched him, real careful – he couldn't have tricked me, and he said lots of magic words and made magic signs and all."
>
> "But there's no such thing as magic!" asserted Sarah. "There's always an explanation – it's like this book I'm reading. These kids got caught in a time warp and they got dragged from the sixteenth century into 1990. Every time they saw a microwave or a TV or something, they thought it was magic, but it isn't, of course – it's all science. They just didn't understand it. Magic is just science or trickery."
>
> "Like the time warp, eh?" Wai Ling countered. "I've read that book. The time warp was created by an evil magician – that's got to be magic. You can't trick people into a time warp, and science can't make one either."
>
> "Oh, but it's just a book," said Sarah. "If there was a real time warp – and maybe there can't be one – then it would have to be part of science. There's no such thing as magic."
>
> "There is," said Wai Ling. "I know there is …", but the bell went just then and they all had to hurry off to morning fitness.

Discussion guides

Acids and alkalis

The science in this story involves two classes of substances – acids and alkalis – and a third class – indicators – which change their colour as the acidity or alkalinity of their environment changes. Explaining how indicators work is quite complicated, and is not usually attempted in science classes at upper primary/lower secondary level. Indeed, indicators are usually treated (but not described!) as if they were magic. Put reasonably simply, acids have excess hydrogen ions, and these react with the indicator to change a part of their molecular structure in a way that affects their ability to absorb and reflect light. Similarly, alkalis contain excess hydroxide ions, which result in a different change to the molecular structure. Whether you need to share this information with your class is up to you, and probably depends on their prior learning.

Science and magic

If we are wondering about science and how it works, it can be useful to contrast science with other activities. Magic is not, of course, a real world activity (unless we are talking about sleight of hand and other illusions). Your students, though, are likely to be very familiar with the idea of magic from fictional sources.

Many writers have been fascinated by magic, and they often have their characters explore its relation to science. In JK Rowling's *Harry Potter and the philosopher's stone* (1997), wizard Arthur Weasley is fascinated by how Muggles (non-magical folk) solve problems scientifically, for which wizards use magic. Terry Pratchett's failed wizard Rincewind, in his Discworld novel *The colour of magic* (1985), similarly wonders whether there is a better way to achieve outcomes than learning long and difficult spells.

Science makes the assumption that all phenomena are explicable in physical terms, and seeks that explanation. This explanation is generally given by describing the mechanism by which things happen. The nature of a magical explanation however is less clear: exploring what magic might be can be a good way of clarifying the nature of a scientific explanation. However, as might be the case with indicators, we may find that the explanations science can offer are beyond our understanding, and they can look like a form of magic. As science fiction giant Arthur C. Clarke's (2000) oft-quoted Third Law puts it: 'Any sufficiently advanced technology is indistinguishable from magic'.

1. If you see something happen and you don't know how it works, does that mean it is magic?
2. If nobody knows how something works, does that mean it is magic?
3. If you saw something and you couldn't possibly imagine how it might work, would that mean it is magic?
4. If you had grown up in 1600 AD and you saw a television set, would you think it was magic?
5. Suppose some aliens landed on earth. They can make amazing things happen. When you ask them how they do it, they say that it is magic. Would you believe them? Or would you think that their science is better than ours?
6. Is magic an explanation for anything? Is science?

Since the demarcation between science and magic seems to rest in the nature of the explanation, the list below starts students thinking about what it is to be able to explain something.

1. If you don't know how something works, how can you find out?
2. If someone tells you how it works, how do you know whether to believe them?
3. If someone tells you how it works, how much do they have to tell you before you understand the explanation?
4. If you do an experiment to find out how it works, how much do you have to find out before you think you have the explanation?
5. What sort of things would someone have to say (or you have to work out) so that it has been explained?
6. Which of the following would be an explanation: a mathematical equation; a 'picture' in your head of how it works; or a law that says it must work like this? What else might an explanation be?

Activity 2 | Sliding Glasses

Emma, Alex and Sarah sat down under a tree to eat their lunch. They'd had a pretty active morning with Physical Education, and later a special soccer lesson with a famous player who had been to the school and run a coaching clinic. So now they just wanted to sit and talk.

"What did you do on the weekend, Sarah?" asked Alex.

"Oh, mum and dad have bought a boat and we went out for a sail," she replied.

"Wow! They must have a lot of money," commented Emma. "Or is it just a little dinghy?"

"No, they don't have heaps of money, but it isn't a dinghy either," answered Sarah. "It's one of those little trailer-sailers. You know, they have a keel like a big yacht, but they're not really that big – just a little cabin below deck."

"What was it like?" Alex wanted to know. "There was a bit of a swell on Friday night when I went surfing. Did you get seasick?"

"It was a bit up and down," admitted Sarah, "but it didn't affect me. Well, not really – I didn't throw up or anything. But we did go below deck to have lunch and we got pretty sick of the glasses sliding across the table. Dad said mum should have 'parked' it behind a headland. Mum told him that real sailors say 'anchored', not 'parked', and he got a bit annoyed. I reckon he was just feeling a bit off because of the waves."

"I hope they didn't have a fight about it. Anyhow, you can solve the glasses sliding about problem easy enough. Just stick something onto the bottom of the glasses so they don't slide so easily," said Emma.

$\longrightarrow$

"Nah, mum and dad were OK," Sarah answered. "But that's a good idea about the glasses. What do you stick on the bottom?"

"I don't know," admitted Emma. "I just heard it somewhere. You could try out a few things – see what's the best, then use that."

The conversation drifted onto another topic then, but later that day, Sarah reflected on the earlier discussion. It was her mum's birthday soon and she thought she'd like to give her mum a surprise by stopping the glasses slipping across the table on the boat. "I guess I'll have to try out some stuff so I know what's best to stick on them," she thought, "but what's the best way to go about that, so I can be sure? I don't want to stick stuff on and then find it's no good."

Discussion guides

Note: this story raises similar issues to Bouncing Balls (see Activity 12), and the discussion guides in that activity may assist you here.

Simplification in scientific experiments

If Sarah wants to find out what the best material is for sticking on the bottom of glasses, she could follow Emma's suggestion and experiment. Does this mean she has to take the boat out, experiment with lots of different materials and test them all out on the water? Well, she could … but it might be easier to simplify the experiment.

1. Could Sarah take the boat out into a swell to test her materials? Would it be the best way to do it? What would the problems be?
2. If Sarah doesn't take the glasses out on the boat, how can she test them?
3. If Sarah decides to do the experiment on land, should she try to make everything just like it would be if she were out on the boat?
4. If not, how can she decide what aspects of the experience of being on a boat need to be reproduced in her experiment?
5. If, for example, she decides to make an artificial swell, how can she ensure it is the same as a real swell? If she doesn't think she needs to make it exactly

the same as a real swell, what is/are the important part(s) of the swell's effects to reproduce?

6. If she makes a realistic swell, how can she ensure that it is exactly the same for each test?

7. Why do we need to simplify experiments in any case?

8. If we simplify a real world situation so that we can do an experiment on it, how can we be sure the results would still work in the real world?

Setting up a fair test

To compare the different materials that might be good on the bottom of the glasses, Sarah will have to ensure that she is comparing like with like. Thus she will have to set up a fair test. There are several steps involved.

Note that the following questions assume students are familiar with the concept of a variable, and the values it can take – and that they understand the distinctions between independent or input variables, dependent or output variables (you can use either set of terms) and controlled variables. If not, then some discussion of these ideas will be needed first.

1. Which variable is the independent/input variable? That is, which variable is the one we are going to investigate for its effect? How can we measure it?

2. Which variable is the dependent/output variable? That is, what are we going to be looking for when we do a series of tests with different values for the independent variable? How can we measure this?

3. Are there any other variables that might be involved in the experiment? Which of these are important (might get in the way of a meaningful experiment), and which can be ignored?

4. Which of the important variables need to be controlled? How can we design the test so that each of the tests are the same in every way except for changes in the one we are testing (the independent/input variable)?

5. Are any of the variables related to each other in a way that might interfere with the experiment?

Criteria for best

Sarah wants to find the best material for stopping the glasses from sliding. This might seem straightforward, but we may be looking for other desirable features as well. For example, superglue would almost certainly stop the glasses sliding, but we might still like to be able to pick them up from the table. Examples of other factors that might need to be taken into consideration include how expensive the chosen material is, how easy it is to get hold of and whether it will stick to the glasses well.

1. What do we mean by the best material to put on the bottom of the glasses? Is the ability to stop the glasses sliding the only relevant factor?
2. If there are other factors, what are they?
3. If we have identified some other factors, how do we decide what importance to place on them?
4. What do we do if we find that some materials are better in some ways we think are important, but worse in others?
5. Is there a single, best material?
6. Do we have to test all possible materials to answer the question?

Follow-up experiment

The obvious experiment to follow-up this discussion would try to investigate what the best material would be to stick on the bottom of a glass to stop it sliding in a swell. However, you may well find that the question the students want to investigate will be a somewhat different one. For example, one class I worked with decided they wanted to ask: "Will a heavy glass start to slide before a lighter glass?" and an even further removed question: "Will heavier objects fall faster than light ones?" Whether you encourage the class to devise an experiment to answer such questions may well depend on how comfortable you feel with running such an experiment – also how practical their suggestions for the design of the experiment will be.

Assuming the students are happy to investigate the main question asked in the story, there is still some work to do. Clearly, the question needs some unpacking in terms of how exactly we would go about carrying out an experiment to answer the question in a classroom. Perhaps the ideal way to go about this is to ask the class to discuss how they are going to test materials. As they discuss, you can intervene to give clues, make suggestions, point out difficulties and gather the thoughts into a method that can be used.

Alternatively, you could ask small groups of students to design an experiment to answer their question (each could choose a different question if you do this) and then submit their design to a research committee (the rest of the class, headed by you), which will ask questions about the thinking behind certain decisions. This can lead to modifications of designs. Once groups have their experimental design settled, they can carry out the experiment.

Each of the discussion guides above highlights some of the issues that will need to be decided: how to simplify the situation so as to make the experiment practical; what variables to test and control; how to measure the variables; and what would count as 'the best' material. Here is a possible experimental design – but your students might well choose a different design.

Variables

Independent variable: the material stuck on the bottom of the glass.

Dependent variable: the angle at which the glass starts to slip.

Variables to be controlled: the type of glass; the volume of contents (if any); the speed at which the glass will travel on the slope.

Method

1. Stick the first material on the bottom of a glass.
2. Place the glass on a board.
3. Smoothly and slowly raise one edge of the board, making sure the other edge can't move.
4. When the glass starts to slip, stop raising the board and measure the angle it makes with the horizontal.
5. Remove the material just tested, stick on the next material and repeat from step 2 (raising the board at the same rate in step 3), until all materials have been tested.

The best material for stopping the glass from slipping is therefore the one that could be raised to the greatest angle before the glass starts to slip. Whether this will turn out to be the best material for keeping the glass from sliding in the much more complex situation of a boat in a swell is, of course, open to question.

Activities 3–5 overview | The light and vision stories

The following three stories all concern light and vision. The problems children have with understanding scientific accounts of everyday phenomena often spring from the fact that they have well-established ways of thinking about those phenomena that rely on what they see and experience. Scientific explanations, on the other hand, often involve a redescription of what we see or experience directly, in terms of things that cannot be directly perceived. A good example is the explanation of the properties of matter in terms of the interactions of atoms and molecules, which are far too small to be seen.

In the following stories, the most important theoretical entity is light. Since, unlike 'atom' or 'molecule', 'light' is an extremely common word, describing something we all experience every day, children are very likely to be confident that they already know what it means.

However, 'light' can mean different things to different people. People, including children, often think of light as:

- a perceptible sensation of brightness. Thus, "The light is shining on the carpet" means that there is a patch of brightness on the carpet.
- a property of space that makes things visible. Thus, "It's light in this room" means that the room is filled with light in the same way that an underwater room might be filled with water.
- an object that makes light. Thus, "Let's have some light in here" is to ask for a torch or other light emitting device to be brought in.

It is worth noting that people who fully understand the scientific account also use these concepts of light in many everyday contexts.

The scientific account of light is quite different from all of these accounts. Light is a form of energy. It is emitted by sources, such as the sun, a torch or a globe. Light travels in straight lines from the source in all directions, and interacts with objects it encounters. Some of the light is absorbed by objects, some is allowed through (by transparent or translucent objects), and some bounces off (i.e., reflects from) objects.

Almost all school science work in light and optics depends on such an understanding of light. Yet children who listen to a teacher describe, say, light shining on an object, can interpret this in terms of their pre-existing notions of light, and fail to draw the intended implication: light travels through space.

The contexts of the three stories in this unit are intended to allow your class to gradually build a more scientific model of light (and related matters) and check it against different situations, each of which reinforces the need for a notion of light as a travelling entity. They deal respectively with blocking the path of light by an opaque object, thus forming a shadow; the diffuse reflection of light by objects towards an eye, enabling vision; and the differences between objects that allow light to pass through unimpeded, partially, or not at all – transparent, translucent and opaque objects respectively.

Activity 3 | Shadow Play

It had been a lovely sunny day, and Emma was walking home with her friend Jenny. The sun was behind them, low in the sky, and the trees looked golden in the late afternoon light. Suddenly they saw a shadow coming, and turned to see Alex quickly creeping up behind them across the grass.

"Drat," he said. "I was trying to sneak up to you and give you a fright. Did you hear me coming? I was trying really hard not to make too much noise."

"No," laughed Jenny, "we didn't hear you. But if you want to sneak up on people, you shouldn't have the sun behind you. We saw your shadow – look how long it is!"

"Oh, yeah, I forgot about that," groaned Alex.

Tom, who was walking along casually about 30 metres behind, shouted "I didn't! That's why I bet you that you couldn't surprise them. And I was right – now you owe me an ice-cream."

"I don't know why it's so long," moaned Alex. "I always thought your shadow was the same size as you."

"Of course it isn't," laughed Jenny. "It depends on where the sun is. But it's always attached to you, unless you're Peter Pan – remember when Wendy had to sew his shadow back on?" (Their class had gone to see the play earlier in the year.)

"I don't think that's right," Emma commented, and then she jumped in the air. "See?"

"No, I don't," Tom complained, but then he said, "Oh, I see what you mean," as she did it again.

"You couldn't really sew a shadow back on, though, could you?" persisted Jenny. "I mean, it isn't anything really, is it? Just a bit of black that follows you around – you can't pick it up like Wendy did. It looked like they used a bit of black cloth to me." And she laughed as much as any of them, as she bent down and pretended to roll her shadow up.

"Hey, you did it!" shouted Alex. "It's gone!" They all laughed again because, sure enough, Jenny's shadow had disappeared as a cloud went over the sun. "But I've got to disappear, too. My mum's expecting me – we're going to that Indonesian shadow play that's on at the hall tonight."

They all realised that it was starting to get cooler and the sun would soon disappear altogether, so they hurried off down the road towards their homes.

Discussion guides

Shadows are evidence that light travels in straight lines from its source. If the path of the light is blocked by an object, the light cannot shine on to the surface behind the object, so it remains (relatively) unilluminated, in contrast to the more brightly lit area around it. Thus a shadow is a lack of illumination, rather than an object in its own right.

Nevertheless, common phrases and stories, as well as repeated experiences, lead us to think of shadows as things. For example, we talk of 'casting a shadow', or 'our shadow follows us', while shadows take on a separate identity in cartoons and stories such as *Peter Pan*. (If your students are not familiar with this story, YouTube has some footage of Peter Pan, his shadow, and Wendy with her needle and thread from the Disney animation at <http://www.youtube.com/watch?v=y0uui_ommLI>.) Even for those who have a scientific understanding of shadow production, the appearance of shadows makes them seem like objects; for children who have not formed an understanding of how light travels, this appearance can overwhelm any attempt to teach the scientific explanation.

1. Can you pick up a shadow?
2. Can your shadow become detached from you? If so, explain.

3. If your shadow is detached from you, could it be sewn back on, like Wendy did with Peter Pan's shadow?

4. When do you have a shadow? What is needed for you to have a shadow?

5. Why does there have to be a bright light? What does the light do?

6. Where does your shadow appear? Is there any connection to where the light is coming from?

7. Can you ever have more than one shadow? If so, explain.

8. If a shadow forms because you block the light, how is it that you can see something that is in the shadow?

9. Is a shadow a thing? Why, or why not?

Exercise: Size, shape and other properties of shadows

This exercise (or something similar) can be used when children disagree about the properties of shadows, such as their size and shape. It is best if such an exercise (or small-scale experiment) arises from the children's discussion and/ or specific predictions, statements or disagreements. The children might well devise similar experiments involving, say, themselves and the sun. In this case, let them try these experiments; but you might find that in order to fully test their predictions and hypotheses, they need to have the flexibility and control that the following method gives.

The three major factors in the size and shape of the shadow are: the relative positions of the light source, object and surface; the shape and (provided the shape stays the same) orientation of the object with respect to the light source; and the orientation and shape of the surface on which the shadow is cast.

The mention of predictions and hypotheses above brings out another point: in the discussion that precedes the experiment, you should strongly encourage children to make specific predictions about what will happen in closely specified conditions. Some children may be reluctant to commit themselves strongly to a prediction – this is a good opportunity to introduce the term 'hypothesis' to label such uncertain predictions. After all, a hypothesis needs to be held tentatively, so it can be revised if this is shown to be necessary because its prediction turns out to be wrong.

Equally, there is a need to follow-up with discussion about what the experiment showed. The basic pattern here is Predict, Observe and Explain – a technique widely used in science education for understanding (White & Gunstone 1992). This method is most likely to be effective, however, when both the prediction and the explanation are co-constructed by the children through discussion, rather than given by the teacher.

Such a process models much more closely the normal operations of experiment and explanation in science than is common in school science, where the teacher poses the question to be answered, specifies the steps of the experiment and often supplies the explanation. Research shows that significant numbers of children consider such 'cook book' science to be boring and meaningless (National Research Council 1997). They do not make the connections between the experiment they are asked to carry out and the scientific knowledge they have to learn.

Preliminary discussion

1. Is your shadow always the same size (and/or shape) as you?
2. Under what conditions does the size/shape of your shadow change?
3. What are the factors that might affect the size or shape of your shadow?
4. Can someone volunteer to design a way to test one of their ideas? How can you make sure this design is really testing the factor you have chosen? (Talk through the details until the class is happy that it will test what it is designed to test.)
5. Can each of you predict exactly how the shadow would change during the test? Write it down, or draw a picture. (Ask each student to do this individually.)
6. What do you think will be the relationship between the positions of the light, the object and the shadow?

Carry out the experiment

You can divide the class into small groups to carry out the test the class has designed.

Suggested equipment (for each group):
- a bright light source (such as a torch)
- a piece of cardboard (about 20 centimetres square)
- a piece of cardboard (about 50 centimetres square)

Using the smaller piece of cardboard, the children can cut out a silhouette of themselves. Now, using the torch as the sun, the silhouette, and the larger piece of cardboard as the ground, they can check out their hypotheses concerning the relative orientations and positions of the light source, object and shadowed surface, by keeping two fixed and varying the third.

Post-experiment discussion

1. Whose predictions were not correct?
2. What did you think would happen?
3. Whose predictions were correct?
4. What did happen?
5. Why do you think the shadow changed in the way that it did?

If you have the time, and if the students are coming up with different ideas, you can devise a number of experiments of this sort, each proposed by a different student, to test what happens when you change a different factor.

Activity 4 | Seeing Things

"Oh, you gave me a fright," said Jenny to her friend Emma, who had just walked in the door. "I saw you walk past the window out of the corner of my eye, and just for a moment I thought you were some sort of monster! Then I realised it was you, not a monster at all."

"Yeah, your eyes can play tricks on you sometimes, can't they," laughed Emma. "It's like when it's nearly dark, sometimes I think I see monsters, too."

"It's worse when it's completely dark." Jenny was smiling too. "Then you can't see anything at all – but you can imagine! Sometimes it really gives me the creeps!"

"But after a while your eyes get used to it, don't they, and then you can see a bit, anyway," said Emma.

"That's not right," objected Jenny. "When it's completely dark – no light at all – then you can't see anything, no matter how long you're there. You've got to have light to see."

"Well, I reckon you can, when your eyes get used to the dark," said Emma, "but let's not argue about it. You can see me well enough now, can't you?"

"Yeah, it's light enough here for that. The sun's shining in the window …"

"But it's not shining on us," interrupted Emma. "It's just shining on the wall over there, but we can see each other anyway."

"The light's everywhere," said Jenny. "It's day, so it's light."

"What are you two rabbiting on about?" asked Jenny's older brother Ray, as he came into the kitchen. "You want the lights on in the middle of the day, or something?"

→

"No," the girls laughed together. "We're just talking about how you can see things, and light and stuff," continued Emma. "If it's light, it helps you to see, doesn't it? But what does the light do?"

"I reckon it's all the light rays bouncing around …" Ray started, but Jenny interrupted him.

"Light ray? I reckon you're heavy, Ray!" she teased, and dodged as he good-naturedly pretended to clip her over the ear, then joked, "You're not going to bounce off me, heavy Ray!"

"I mightn't," he went on, "but the light is, right now. Can't you feel it?"

"No, I can't. Is that because it's too light?" They all laughed.

"Light bouncing? You're so funny, Ray," Emma smiled. "Light can't bounce off things! It just shines on them, and lights them up."

"Then how does your eye see them?" asked Ray. "The light has to get into your eye, so it has to bounce off things to get there, that's what I think."

"Well I don't. You just look at it – the sight goes out to the thing, that's how you see it," countered Emma. "That's right, isn't it, Jenny?"

"Oh, I don't know. I'm all confused," wailed Jenny. "I've never seen light move, or bounce, or anything. I've never felt it bounce either. But they're always talking about the speed of light, aren't they? So I guess it must move. And I don't know what you mean by light getting into the eye, Ray. It would blind you, wouldn't it? Like when we flashed the light off your watch into Mrs Sharkey's eyes, remember, Em?"

But Ray was off. "Sorry, can't stay. Tell mum I've gone to Sam's, Jen. I'd better rush, 'cos he's waiting for me," he yelled back over his shoulder as he walked out the door. "Anyhow, you'll see I'm right one day."

"I can see already," retorted Emma, "and I can see I'm right!" The girls laughed again as Ray disappeared up the drive.

Discussion guides

Explaining how we see

Building a scientific explanation of sight involves a series of revisions of naïve theories, and it takes some time to develop the explanation (Collis et al. 1998;

Jones et al. 1997; Sprod & Jones 1997). This story builds on an understanding (which may have been established by Activity 3: Shadow Play, but is revisited here) that light is emitted by light sources and travels in straight lines, and the story introduces two further concepts: that light interacts with many objects by reflecting off them; and that light reflected from an object has to enter the eye in order for sight to work (and hence, in the dark, you can't see).

The nature of light

Light, which bounces off an object, can bounce (or reflect) in one of two ways. It is not uncommon for children to have some understanding of the first way, yet deny that the second way can happen. The two ways are:

1 If the surface is shiny, all the light coming from the same place bounces off in the same direction ('specular reflection'). These are objects like mirrors, shiny metals and so on. Because of this, you are able to see images reflected in such surfaces.

2 The second type of reflection scatters light in all directions off the surface ('diffuse reflection'). Typically, some wavelengths (i.e., colours) of the light hitting the object are absorbed, so the scattered light is of a particular colour and hence carries information about the object. Some of this scattered light enters the eye, then the eye and brain process and interpret the information and we see the object.

Without a concept of light as an entity that moves through space and interacts with objects in the ways already outlined, children are not able to understand the explanation for seeing (see point 2 above). However, coming to understand this involves the children in thinking about light in a different way. The accounts of light Emma and Jenny give – brightness, the condition under which things are visible, bright objects – are merely descriptions of the perceptible effects of light, drawn from direct experience. Ray's account (see point 2 above) involves building a mental model with explanatory power. You can't directly perceive light particles or rays.

As we have seen through a number of stories, building a scientific mental model involves thinking about the world in a different way. No longer is it true that 'what you see is what is'. In order for these new models of the world to take their place in a child's understanding of physical processes, they have to 'make sense' in order to provide a more powerful and fruitful way of thinking about the world. Very often, just being told about them is not enough. Children need time to explore the idea, to see how it leads to a better explanation of events so they can fit the new way of thinking into their old ideas.

1. What does Jenny think light is?
2. What does Ray think light is?
3. What do you think light is?
4. When Emma says the sunlight is shining on the wall, what does she mean?
5. When sunlight shines on the wall, does that mean something is coming from the sun to the wall?
6. If light is something that comes from the sun to the wall, what does it do when it gets to the wall?
7. If light has a speed, does that mean it has to travel?
8. Can light bounce off things? What sort of things? Mirrors? Watch faces? People? Walls?

Follow-up exercise

The different meanings of the word 'light'

In order to alert your students to the many ways 'light' can be used, and the fact that we have different understandings of light in different contexts, you could ask them to identify the meaning of light in the following sentences:

Jenny says: "It is light in this room."

Emma says: "The light is shining on the wall."

Ray says: "You want the light on."

Jenny says: "You're not light, Ray!"

Ray's mum says: "It's hot! I'd love a light beer!"

Emma says: "I want to light the candle. Have you got a light?"

Mrs Sharkey says: "The light is in my eyes! I can't see!"

Jenny's dad says: "I like the way Jenny's eyes light up when I say we're eating at the fish shop tonight."

Ray says: "I think I'll wear my light blue shirt today."

Jenny says: "The speed of light is 300 million metres per second."

Emma says: "Feathers are light, compared to metals."

Can any of your students think of sentences in which light is used with a meaning different from any of these?

Seeing in the dark

We all experience our eyes 'getting used to the dark', as Emma says. Many children do not realise, however, that this is merely our eyes becoming able to use low light. They take the phrase literally, and think that we could eventually see – in the complete absence of light – in the real dark.

1. Do your eyes get used to the dark?
2. Can you always see in the dark if you wait long enough?
3. Have you ever been in complete darkness? Where were you? Could you see after waiting long enough?
4. Do you have to have some light in order to be able to see?
5. How could we test our answer?

Follow-up experiment

Clearly, this matter can be decided by a simple experiment – putting your class in absolute darkness. However, it is not all that easy to find a completely dark place in the course of a school day. Deep in a cave is ideal, but hardly practical. Perhaps you can come up with a more feasible solution.

Light and the eye

One of the more difficult ideas that needs to be grasped, in order to understand the full scientific explanation of sight, is the fact that light, reflected off an object, has to enter the eye. Note that there has to be a prior recognition that light travels out from light sources, and can reflect off any object, before your students can even start grasping this final concept. There are two everyday experiences that can interfere with such an understanding.

First, sight seems to us to be an active, not a passive, process. We have to look at an object in order to see it. Building on this, it is easy to think that the eye causes the seeing of the object, probably by sending something (sight?) out to the object. We look at the object, and we see it. If the eye is a passive receptor, merely requiring light to enter the eyes, so the implicit reasoning goes, then the eyes don't actively see.

Of course, there is an element of truth in this naïve understanding. Indeed, we do have to take action to see a particular object by turning our eye, and hence our attention, towards it. Once attention has been directed properly, though, the eye is passive, merely detecting the light that impinges on it.

The second experience that can interfere with a sophisticated understanding is that of getting 'light in our eyes'. If we glance at the sun, or someone shines a strong light source into our eyes, we are temporarily blinded. Again there seems to be an implicit argument here – if getting light in our eyes blinds us, it can't be how we see. In fact, it is not because light enters the eye, but that the quantity of light is so overwhelming it blinds us.

1. Does your sight go out to the thing you see, as Emma says?
2. Does light bounce off things and then go into your eye so you can see, as Ray says?
3. If light gets in your eye, would it blind you, like Jenny says?
4. How could we decide between the theory that sight goes out to an object to see it, or that light goes into your eyes when you see something?
5. If light coming into the eye lets us see a chair, why do we have to look at the chair before we can see it?
6. If light coming into the eye allows us to see things, why can light in our eyes blind us?

Activity 5 | Super Vision

Alex's little sister Sally was waiting impatiently. Her friend Ian was late, and she had on her new Superman costume to show him. "What's the time now, Alex?" she repeatedly shouted.

"You can tell the time, Sally," Alex replied from the next room, not without a note of annoyance in his voice. "Why don't you just look at the clock?"

"I can't see it from here! There's a wall in the way!" Sally complained.

"Well, move so you can!" Alex sighed. "And anyway, that's no excuse – you're Superman, so you can see through walls."

But Alex's reply was cut off by Sally, who yelled with excitement. Through the window she had seen Ian coming up the path with his older sister Emma. She rushed to open the door.

"Wow, Superman!" Ian was obviously impressed by Sally's outfit.

"I could see you coming through the wall, 'cos I'm Superman and I've got X-ray vision," Sally boasted. "And you're late! I know 'cos I can see the clock in the hall and it says …" [she paused to think what Alex had told her] ten past four!"

Ian rushed wide-eyed into the hall, and sure enough he found a clock saying a little after ten past four. "Gee," he exclaimed, "could I do that if I was wearing your Superman suit?"

"Course you could. You'd be Superman too then."

"Well, let me," demanded Ian. "I wanna see through walls too!"

"No! It's my cape and I haven't used it enough yet." Then, seeing the look of disappointment on Ian's face, Sally conceded, "Maybe I'll let you wear it tomorrow."

$\longrightarrow$

Alex, who had been exchanging amused glances with Emma, winked at her and said, "Gee, I'm impressed, Sally. Can you tell me the colour of the car parked out on the street?"

"Sure," answered Sally, and she rushed to the window. "It's blue!"

Emma and Alex were laughing by now. "I can see through walls, too," spluttered Emma, "when they've got windows in them!"

"Huh," Sally frowned, annoyed at being laughed at. "Let's go to my room, Ian – you can wear my Batman mask if you want." And with that, the two youngsters rushed out.

"What do you reckon, Em? Could it be possible to have X-ray vision for real? You know, see through walls and stuff – with special glasses or something?"

"I'm not sure, Alex," Emma replied. "They do use X-rays to look inside things we can't see into, like when I broke my arm last year, but I remember them telling me that X-rays are very dangerous – they put everything, apart from my arm, behind a lead-lined shield to protect me from them. So I don't think it would be much good letting them anywhere near your eyes."

"Well, they use infra-red glasses to see in the dark, don't they? But I guess the dark isn't like a solid wall. You can see through some solid things, though – like the window."

"Yeah, and there are other things you can sort of see through, like the frosted glass on our front door – you can see someone's there, but you can't tell who they are."

"That's right," said Alex. "Or like our door – it's got stained glass and if you look through one bit, they look all red, but through another bit they're all green and stuff. But I'm hungry. Are you staying? We could have some of that cake dad made."

"Yeah, I'm staying … and I'd love some cake – your dad's a really good cook, isn't he? Mum told me I had to stay and help you supervise Ian and Sally – she's picking us up after work."

"Supervise, eh?" joked Alex. "Sally's got super vision already – she said so!" And they both laughed as they headed for the kitchen.

Discussion guides

Light and objects

The purpose of this story is to get students thinking about how light interacts with different sorts of objects. In Shadow Play (see Activity 3), the idea that light travels through space was introduced. There, the focus was mainly on objects that block light, that is, opaque objects, and how they thus cast a shadow. In this story, attention is turned also on objects that allow light to pass through them, that is, transparent and translucent objects.

In considering that we cannot see through opaque objects, but we must move until we get a clear 'line of sight', the idea that light travels in a straight line will be revisited. However, it should be noted that a line of sight is also compatible with sight as something that goes out from the eye to 'capture' the object. This misconception is considered in more detail in *Seeing Things*. However, the bright patches that sunlight makes when it shines through a window are not explicable in terms of the movement of anything from the patch to the sun. Thus it can reinforce the idea of light travelling from a light source to an object: the first step in realising that light then reflects from the object into the eye (see Activity 4: Seeing Things).

How far you can take this discussion probably depends on your students. Helping them to understand that the difference between opaque, translucent and transparent objects lies in whether (and to what extent) they allow light to pass through them as the key idea, as well as some reinforcement of the idea that light travels in straight lines. If the discussion arises from your students, you might also be able to discuss what can happen when light hits an object (see questions 8 and 9 below): some might pass through the object, some light can reflect (even from transparent objects like windows), and some light may be absorbed. This latter fact explains why objects and glass can be coloured (light of certain colours is absorbed, while other colours reflect or pass through), but it is a quite sophisticated idea, relying on the knowledge that white light is a mixture of different coloured light.

1. Can Sally see through walls?
2. Could Superman see through walls?
3. Why does Sally have to move so that she can see the clock?

4. Can Sally see through windows?
5. What is the difference between a wall and a window?
6. Could you ever see through a wall?
7. Why can you see through some windows clearly, but things are distorted or coloured through other windows?
8. Does all the light pass through a transparent object like a window? How do you know?
9. Does all the light reflect from an opaque object? How do you know?

Possible and impossible

Superhero stories often rely on super powers which are scientifically impossible. Superman can fly, see through solid objects and so on, unaided by technology. Some heroes like Batman do not have super powers, but rely on highly honed skills that we all have, augmented by technological gadgets.

The mention of technology reminds us that what might be impossible for the unaided human (flying, seeing through solid objects) may be perfectly possible when aided by some human invention: planes, or X-ray scanners. Yet there seem to be limits to human technology as well. It might well be impossible to invent a machine to allow us to 'leap tall buildings in a single bound'. The acceleration required might be too great for humans to bear, and the force needed could smash pavements rather than propel us upwards. In other words, the laws of biology and physics may be such as to rule out the possibility.

There is also logical impossibility. It is impossible, for example, to draw a square circle because a figure made of four equal straight lines meeting at right angles cannot be a curved line that is always equidistant from the same point. The two objects have incompatible definitions. Another famous example applies to the idea of an all-powerful God; can He build an object so heavy that He can't lift it? If we say yes, He is not all-powerful (there is something He can't lift). If we say no, again He is not all-powerful (there is something He can't build).

This consideration may lead us to thinking that an all-powerful being need not be required to be able to do anything that is logically impossible. So, there are three types of impossibility:

• Practical impossibility – things are impossible to do, given the state of the world at the moment (you can't travel to the moon for a holiday).

- Physical impossibility – things which are imaginable, perhaps using technology, but which violate physical laws or constraints (precognition, that is, seeing future events).
- Logical impossibility – things which can't even be coherently imagined (a square circle, for example).

What is practically impossible now could quite conceivably be possible in the future. Indeed, scientific and technological advances are making things that were practically impossible into actualities all the time. However, it isn't always easy to tell whether some events are practical or physical impossibilities. Take teleportation: we certainly can't teleport from Australia to England now, but it does seem that (after considerable technological work) it might just conceivably be possible one day. However, there may be some physical law or constraint that we have not yet thought through properly – or even discovered – that will turn out to make it physically impossible.

Similarly, the discovery of a different set of scientific laws (as happened when Albert Einstein replaced Newton's Laws with the Theory of Relativity) might one day show that things we think physically impossible are indeed possible. History is littered with examples of new discoveries, embarrassing distinguished scientists who have declared that such-and-such is physically impossible. You might encourage your students to look for examples.

1. Is it possible that Sally could see through walls?
2. Might a scientist invent a machine that allows us to see through walls?
3. In the comics and movies, Superman can fly. Is that possible?
4. Is it possible that you could fly?
5. Can you think of any examples of things that were not possible in the past, but are possible now?
6. Can you think of any examples of things that are not possible now, but will definitely be possible within a few years?
7. Can you think of any examples of things that are not possible now, but might be possible a long way into the future?
8. Can you think of any examples of things that will never be possible? Why not?
9. Do you know of any examples of things that people in the past said would never be possible, but which we now do or have?

Activity 6 | Are Scientists Mad?

"I saw a great movie last night," Jenny enthused as they all sat eating their lunches. "It was about this secret organisation that wanted to take over the world."

"I saw that too," Andy almost shouted. "Wasn't it great the way the hero was the only one who knew what they were trying to do, and nobody believed her – they all thought she was crazy."

"Yeah, but the one that was really crazy was the mad scientist," Conchita reckoned. "He had invented a machine that could blow up a whole city from space, and it was lucky she got there in time to stop them."

"Why would you do that?" asked Alex.

"Did you want them to blow up Sydney?" Conchita interjected angrily.

"No, no – I didn't mean that," Alex hastily corrected. "I meant why would you want to invent something that could destroy a city?"

"'Cos he was crazy, that's why," Andy opined. "You'd have to be crazy to do that."

"He certainly was crazy in the movie," Luigi put in, "but what about all those scientists that invent weapons? What about the guys who invented the atom bomb? Were they all crazy?"

"Yeah, and all those guns and mines and, and … I heard about a bomb that, when it hits the ground, it just throws out lots of sharp bits of metal that cut up anyone nearby. Why would you want to invent something as horrible as that?" Jenny was clearly getting upset.

"That's scientists for you," Greta stated. "Think of all the nasty things they have invented, like GM food and cloning. I reckon they're all mad!"

"Yeah, and medicines and computers and solar energy," added Luigi. "It isn't all bad!"

"But that's what I was getting at," continued Alex. "Some stuff scientists do is good – lots of it, I guess – but some scientists just work on things that couldn't possibly be good, like horrible weapons. Why do they do that?"

"I bet they don't even think about whether it's good or bad. I reckon they just love to invent things, and they get carried away," Jenny said.

"Or they are just trying to understand how stuff works," added Luigi. "I was reading about Albert Einstein, and it said that he invented the atom bomb, sort of. At least, he worked out that equation – you know, $E=mc^2$ – and they used that to make the bomb. And he was a pacifist!"

"So, you reckon that the scientists are just doing science, do you," asked Greta, "and that it isn't their fault if other people make weapons out of it? I think if they know that what they're doing can be used for bad stuff, they shouldn't do it."

"So some science shouldn't be done at all," mused Alex. "Who decides which is right?"

Discussion guides

Science and social responsibility

I have to admit that the inspiration for this story came from Fredric Brown's 'The Weapon' (2001). This beautifully constructed short story may be a better one to read with your class than mine – you can source the text on the web.

Scientific advances, as the characters in my story recognise, can be used for good purposes or bad. However, this is not a straightforward issue, because it is not always obvious that a particular piece of scientific research will lead to either good or bad outcomes. This is particularly true when the research is what might be called 'basic', 'pure' or 'fundamental'. In such research, scientists are looking for the underlying laws or explanations, with little or no expectation that there will be any specific practical applications of what they find.

The research conducted by Albert Einstein and many others into Relativity and its implications is a good example of such pure research. It was only when much of the basic science had been done that the realisation dawned that there was a potential to release vast amounts of energy. Even then, the suggestions for its use varied from good (cheap energy, when the potential dangers of nuclear reactions were much less well understood) to bad (the atomic bomb). As Luigi comments in the story, even this last judgement is not straightforward: Einstein, though a pacifist, urged the US development of the atom bomb because he felt it to be a lesser evil than Nazi Germany developing it. (If you are interested in the full story, Robert Jungk's *Brighter than a thousand suns* (1958) makes fascinating reading, and there are many other retellings.)

The distinction between pure and applied research is useful. In applied research, the scientists involved have a clear practical use for their research in mind, and we can then make a moral judgement about their aim. It seems pretty clear that searching for a good way to wipe out malaria, for example, is morally good research, while we may have more moral qualms about the search for a more efficient way to kill enemies in war. There is another distinction that might arise – between applied science and technology – though the two are not as easily separable as they once might have been.

Most scientific research and application today involves many people. It is very rare for a single scientist to discover new scientific knowledge and to develop a device in isolation. Hence, we can ask what moral responsibilities each of the persons involved in the process must bear. Notice that, while the following questions concentrate on weapons, they could easily be adapted to other uses of science mentioned in the story.

1. If a scientist discovers a new effect, and uses it to design a new way of killing people, are they a bad person?
2. If a scientist discovers a new effect, and somebody else uses it to design a new way of killing people, is the scientist a bad person?
3. Does it make a difference whether the scientist knew in advance that it was likely their work could be used to make a new weapon?
4. Is a scientist wrong if they don't think about how their work might be used?

5. Is it always good to discover new knowledge, or is there some knowledge that should not be sought?
6. If there are some sorts of knowledge that people should not try to find, what are some examples?
7. If scientific knowledge is used in ways we judge to be immoral, should we blame the following:
   - The scientist(s) who discovered that knowledge?
   - The scientists or technologists who developed the way it was used?
   - The person(s) who paid for the development?
   - The politicians who didn't ban it?
   - All citizens, for not putting pressure on politicians to ban it?

Activity 7 | Energy

"You've got plenty of energy," said Jenny, as Maeve ran past at full tilt. Maeve slowed down, circled back and collapsed on the bench next to Jenny and Emma, who were sharing a bag of popcorn.

"I don't think so," she managed to pant out after a few moments, catching her breath. "I don't feel like I've got any energy left at all!"

"Why are you doing so much running anyway?" asked Jenny. "I saw you out yesterday and again this morning."

"I'm just running to get fit for hockey," replied Maeve. "We start the season next week and I'll need all the energy I can get."

"But you just said that you're out of energy," Emma butted in. "How can you have more when you play hockey if you use it all up running now?"

"Well," panted Maeve, "if I get fit now, I'll certainly be better for it next week. Last year, I didn't do any pre-season training and I completely ran out of puff by half-time. And my muscles were really sore after the game."

"Yeah, I know what you mean," said Jenny. "I come up better if I'm fit before the netball season starts. But it's strange, what you just said. Does getting fit give you more energy, or does it use it up?"

"It must give you more," said Emma. "After all, where else would it come from? You said it yourself – if you're fit, you always feel like you've got more energy … Do you want any popcorn?" she added, seeing the way Maeve was staring at the bag.

"Yeah, great," said Maeve, holding out her hand. "I'm always starved after I've been for a run. Dad says I eat like a horse in the hockey season."

"That's probably where all the energy comes from," Jenny put in. "Mum always says food is like fuel for the body, and cars get their energy from fuel, don't they? That's what makes them go, and it probably makes you go, too."

"So I should drink a cup of petrol before the game, hey?" laughed Maeve, and they all joined in at the thought of this. Then she settled down and said, "Yeah, I guess there's energy in food – see, they've got it on the side of the packet: Energy, so many kilojoules per 100 grams. How do they work that out, I wonder?"

"Yeah, I wonder too. And I wonder how getting fit gives you more energy, if you use it up getting fit … and I wonder how the body gets the energy from food – it can't just light a little fire in your stomach, can it? And anyway, foods don't burn like fuels, do they?" Emma was lost in thought.

"Well, gotta run, as they say," shouted Maeve, getting up. "Thanks for the popcorn. I've got my energy back, so I'll do some more training. See ya," and off she ran.

Discussion guides

Energy is a key concept in all the sciences, yet it is a somewhat slippery one for students to grasp. Partly, this is because it is also a word in common usage, and that usage does not always conform to the scientific meaning. Yet, even in the sciences, it is not always used consistently – at least, not in the contexts that students will hear it. The standard physics definition is the capacity to do work, yet 'work' is also a common word with a specific scientific meaning: it involves the exertion of a force in moving an object. Sitting quietly and thinking hard may seem like hard work, but in physics terms, little work is done. In biology, geology and many other sciences, energy is more commonly associated with change than work.

Energy is such a key scientific concept, and there are so many ways it enters into different scientific contexts, that the aim of this story is not to get the concept straight in the students' minds once and for all, but rather to assist them to become aware that it is important, and that they will need to pay close attention to how it is being used, as they deepen their knowledge.

Different meanings of words – scientific and common usage

1. What different meanings can you think of for the word 'energy'?
2. Which is the right meaning?
3. Does the 'right' meaning of a word depend on the context in which we use it?
4. How does an everyday word get its meaning?
5. How does a scientific word get its meaning?
6. Why are scientific words different from everyday words?
7. Would it be better if scientists used new words for their specialised meanings, rather than changing the meaning of everyday words?

Does exercise increase your energy or use it up?

In everyday life, there is a usage of 'energy' which can run counter to any scientific understanding, and that is the sense of energy as 'get up and go', or enthusiasm. In this sense, our 'energy levels' can be raised by exercise or other activities, which always use up energy in the scientific sense.

1. Does Maeve have plenty of energy when she sits down with Jenny and Emma?
2. Is Maeve using up energy or building up energy while she is running?
3. Does getting fit give you more energy?
4. If energy doesn't come from being fit, what does fitness do for you?
5. If energy doesn't come from being fit, where does it come from?
6. Did Maeve get her energy back from the rest she had, or did she get something else back?
7. Is food like a fuel? How?
8. Is the word 'energy' being used in different ways by different characters in this story? What ways?

The nature of energy

Science can be seen as the study of matter and energy. While students have little difficulty understanding the nature of matter, since they handle it all the time, energy is less obvious. It is most easily experienced through its effects, but since it is not visible, it can be hard to trace where it goes, or whether it is used up and disappears. Eventually, students will learn that energy can change forms as it acts, but it is conserved – the total amount of energy does not change. It is unlikely that students will come to this full realisation yet, but they can start to consider what energy is.

1. Does Maeve need energy to be able to run?
2. Think of the various things that you do. Which do you need energy for?
3. Does Emma need energy to think?
4. If Maeve uses energy when she runs, what happens to it? Does it disappear?
5. Does energy get used up?
6. What is energy?

Energy storage and energy release – types of energy

Energy comes in different forms. In food and in fuel, it is stored in chemical compounds as chemical energy. Chemical reactions in the body release that energy for various purposes. In the muscles, the energy is converted into movement as Maeve runs – kinetic energy – and the heat that makes her hot as she exercises. By carrying out our own chemical reaction – by burning the food – we can attempt to measure the energy contained in the food.

1. Is there energy in food?
2. Is there energy in fuels, like petrol?
3. What makes food and fuels have energy?
4. How can we use the energy in a fuel?
5. What happens to the energy in food when you eat it?
6. How could we find out if food does contain energy?
7. How can the energy content of food be measured?
8. What sorts of energy does Maeve have when she is running?
9. Are there different types of energy? What are they?

Follow-up experiment: Popcorn

In the original version of this story, the children were eating peanuts, but the fact that many schools now ban peanuts (on allergy grounds) meant I had to rewrite it. Peanuts burn very well (longer than popcorn!) and could be used in the experiment if your school would allow it – but lots of other foods will do, such as baked savoury biscuits, potato chips, breakfast cereals, pasta and so on.

The experiment below is set out in a formal way, but you can, of course, modify it in any way you like for your class. It also assumes you have access to science equipment. If you are in a primary school that doesn't have access, you might approach your nearest high school for a loan of science equipment. Alternatively, you can substitute more readily available objects, such as a small jar for a test tube.

Some suggested modifications:

- Test a number of different foods (check to see they will burn adequately first!).
- Work out the energy content of popcorn per 100 grams by weighing the popcorn first. (You will need sensitive scales, or you could weigh a large number of popcorn pieces, or even the corn before it is popped – say 100 pieces – and calculate the weight of one piece from that.) Compare it to the figure on the packet.
- Start off by making your own popcorn.

Measuring the energy in food

Aim: to measure the energy content of popcorn.

Group size: Divide the class into groups of three. Within these groups each student will have a different role: recorder, test tube handler or measurer.

Equipment the group requires:
- a candle
- a thermometer (0°C to 100°C)
- a test tube (or similar container) around 50 millilitre capacity
- a test tube holder (can be made out of a sheet of paper – fold it lengthways into a narrow band, and wrap it once around the test tube, holding the ends together)
- a long needle, or something similar that can be stuck into the popcorn so it can be held without getting burnt (a straightened paperclip is a good substitute)
- two or more pieces of popcorn, stuck on the needle.

Equipment the class requires:

- a bag of popcorn – probably best if it does not have a sugary coating, which could possibly melt rather than burn (butter is fine)
- access to water
- measuring cylinders graduated in millilitres, so that 20 millilitres can be measured fairly easily (a medicine cup will do)
- matches.

Method:

1. *Measurer*: measure out 20 millilitres of water. Pour it into the test tube, which is held in the test tube holder by the test tube handler. *Recorder*: write down how much water was used.
2. *Measurer*: use the thermometer to measure the temperature of the water. *Recorder*: write it down. Leave the thermometer in the tube.
3. *Recorder*: light the candle. *Measurer*: hold the popcorn at the top of the flame just long enough to get it burning. When it is burning, hold it under the test tube, which is held by the test tube handler. Keep the popcorn under the test tube until it goes out.
4. *Measurer*: when the popcorn has burnt up completely, measure the temperature of the water. *Recorder*: write it down. Test tube handler: carefully pour the water out of the test tube and clean it. (Beware – it will be hot!)
5. *Recorder*: with the help of the others and using the information on the Recorder's Sheet, calculate the energy content of the popcorn.

Recorder's Sheet:

Amount of water used: _____ mL

Temperature of the water at the start: _____ °C

Temperature of the water at the end: _____ °C

Information: In order to heat up 1 millilitre of water by 1 degree Celsius, you need 4.2 joules of energy. (A joule (symbol: J) is a measure of energy, in this case, heat energy.)

How much energy, measured in joules, did the popcorn contain? _____J

How did you work it out?

Follow-up discussion

Accuracy of experiments and experimental design

Years ago, when doing this experiment with a lower secondary class, before I had written the story, I casually asked a student how accurate their answer was. The answer was that it was very accurate, because they had used a calculator. (Their answer ran to several decimal places.)

In fact, this experiment gives a very inaccurate answer. It assumes that all the energy the popcorn originally contained is transferred to the water. There are many ways in which the energy isn't transferred. Some energy is lost when lighting the popcorn. Some of it heats the glass, not the water. Much of it heats the air around the test tube. The popcorn may not have burned completely. Your students will no doubt think of other problems (including measurement errors), once they get the idea.

1. How accurate is your calculation of the energy content of the popcorn?
2. What are some of the factors that make this experiment inaccurate?
3. Why would a scientist do an experiment if they knew the answer was going to be inaccurate?
4. How could a scientist make this experiment accurate?
5. Could a scientist ever make this experiment completely accurate?
6. Why do students in a science class do experiments when the answer is going to be inaccurate?
7. Why didn't we do a really accurate experiment such as the one we thought up for a scientist to do?

Calculation

Finally, you might explore the role of calculation in this experiment. As students move up through the years in science classes, they will find that they need to draw more and more on mathematics: even sciences which were once much more descriptive (like biology) use mathematical tools much more frequently now.

How much you want to explore the connection between science and mathematics probably depends a lot on how advanced your students' mathematics is. The third question below, for example, depends on them understanding algebra to some extent.

1. How did you work out the energy content of the popcorn?
2. Why did it work?
3. Could you write an equation that allowed you to work out the energy content of any food, provided you used the method we used here?
4. If our experiment is not very accurate, why bother to try to work out a figure for the amount of energy?
5. Why do scientists try to work out amounts (like the amount of energy in popcorn) rather than just why things happen?
6. What's the relationship between science and mathematics?

Activity 8 | Dinosaurs

"I saw a great program on TV last night," Sarah enthused. "It was called *Walking with dinosaurs*, and it had all this great stuff showing dinosaurs eating, fighting and even hatching these cute little dinosaur babies."

"Yeah, I saw that," said Tom. "What I couldn't figure out was how they got the cameras back there."

"Don't be silly, Tom – it wasn't real."

"You mean it was all lies?" asked Tom, in mock disgust. "I thought they must have invented a time machine."

"Oh, stop it, Tom. You're just pulling my leg," realised Sarah. "I guess it's just all sorts of clever models and computer animation and stuff. But that doesn't mean that it's lies. It's just like it would have been, if you had been around then."

"Are you sure?" Tom demanded. "How could they possibly know what it was like way back then?"

"Well, they're scientists, aren't they – or anyway, the people who made it asked the scientists who know all about it. And anyway, that was right back in the days of cavemen, wasn't it? They probably drew pictures of it on cave walls and stuff."

Tessa had been silent and listening, but this was too much. "Come on! Dinosaurs were around long before the cavemen – millions of years earlier. My mum said so."

Sarah pouted. "Oh well, who cares?" she asked. "It's still true, because the scientists say so."

"I'm not so sure it was all true, but it probably wasn't all lies either," asserted Tessa. "I mean, how could they possibly know all that? I can see that they could have known some stuff, like what sort of shape the dinosaurs were, but they must have just guessed some of the rest. How could you tell what colour they were, for example?"

"Yeah, or what those mummy dinosaurs did with their kids," interjected Andy. "Anyway, I just don't get how those people who study dinosaurs can be real scientists. I mean, scientists do experiments, don't they? What sort of experiments could you do with animals that lived long ago? I reckon it's more like ancient history."

"Of course it's science," said Tom, heatedly. "They're called palaeontologists, aren't they – and that's science – everybody calls it science."

"I see what you mean, Tessa" put in Sarah. "Remember what Mr Carey told us – about the scientific method – you know, controlling variables and stuff. That's what makes it science. You can't do that to stuff in the past, can you?"

"Well, Mr Carey could be wrong, couldn't he?" countered Tom. "I mean, he talked to us once about scientists called palaeontologists who study fossils. I reckon anyone who gets called a scientist must be doing science."

"I'm confused now," wailed Sarah. "Let's just ask Mr Carey in science – we've got it after lunch. I gotta run now – see you later!" And off she ran.

Discussion guides

Evidence, reason and imagination

Science is often portrayed as a purely rational process. However, in most (arguably all) parts of science the evidence does not lead by a purely rational process to the answer. Sometimes, as in this case, it is obvious that not all the possible evidence is available. However, even in laboratory science, other experiments could be done, other evidence could be collected, or several explanations might be possible. Scientists have to use their imagination – to go beyond the evidence, to think up hypotheses to test, to work out ways of explaining the evidence. Students should be aware of the important role of imagination in science, and consider how far to go with imagination.

1. How did the makers of *Walking with dinosaurs* know what it was like so many millions of years ago?
2. Which sorts of facts about dinosaurs are easiest to find out? How?
3. What sorts of evidence of the past are we most likely to find? Why?
4. If we want to know about something from the past, and the evidence that has survived isn't complete, how can we work out what it was like?
5. What role does reason play in going beyond the evidence?
6. What role do imagination and speculation play in going beyond the evidence?
7. Documentaries like this present lots of information as if it were factual and solid. Should people who make guesses that go beyond the evidence have to tell others where they have made guesses, and how well supported they are?
8. Can a scientist let their imagination go too far? How far is too far?

Scientific method(s)

Students are often taught the 'scientific method' – it frequently appears in science textbooks. Yet the method given is often very heavily based on laboratory experiments, drawn from physics and chemistry. Many other scientists find it hard, even impossible, to carry out many experiments. This might be because the events they study are too far away in time (fossils) or space (astrophysics), too large (meteorologists) or too complex (ecosystems). It might be that an experiment can be designed, but to carry it out would be unethical.

1. Could scientists who study dinosaurs do experiments on them? If so, how? If not, why not?
2. Do scientists have to do experiments?
3. Can you think of any other methods scientists use apart from experiments?
4. Can you think of any other types of science, apart from palaeontology, that don't use experiments?
5. Is there a single scientific method, or are all methods used by scientists therefore scientific?

Humans and dinosaurs

It is not an uncommon belief (as for Sarah in the story) that humans and dinosaurs co-existed. After all, many fictional entertainments (e.g., *The Flintstones*) reinforce this idea. Of course, sorting out when humans first appeared and when dinosaurs disappeared is not merely a matter for discussion. If any impasse should arise in discussion about the facts of the matter, there are excellent opportunities for research projects. Sorting out what might count as reliable sources and methods can be a useful precursor to such research.

Any research students do on the dating of the rise and fall of dinosaurs, and the evolution of humans, will result in figures of many millions of years. It is not easy to get a grasp of just how vast geological time is. The timeline activity below can, in a hands-on way, start students thinking about these timescales.

1. Was there a time when humans and dinosaurs were both alive?
2. How could you find out if they were or they weren't?
3. If we look it up in a book or online, how can we tell whether the book or website is reliable or not?
4. If people disagree about the answer, how can we sort out who is right?
5. If you wanted to work out for yourself whether they were or weren't right, how would you go about it?
6. How do the experts – those who write books and websites – work out the answers they give?
7. If you find there are different methods used by different people, how can we decide which method is best?

Follow-up activities

1. Walking with Dinosaurs

The students in this story are referring to the six-part television documentary mini-series, *Walking with dinosaurs* (BBC, 1999), first broadcast in the UK and subsequently shown in many other countries. Many schools will have a DVD copy. The following activity can be done using *Walking with dinosaurs*, or (with a little modification) any other scientific pseudo-documentary, such as others in the BBC's *Walking with* … series. I suggest that you:

- Hand out the worksheet (see below and also <http://www.acer.edu.au/discussions-in-science>) and explain that students should fill in the table in Part 1 as they are watching the DVD.
- Show the first 14 minutes of Episode 5: Spirits of the ice forest.
- Put students in pairs to discuss the questions in Part 2 of the worksheet and the table.
- Bring the class back into a community of inquiry to discuss their ideas.
- If internet access is available, students can access what the documentary makers had to say about making this episode online (see link below).

Discuss how legitimate the use of evidence, reasoning, conjecture and imagination in the *Walking with dinosaurs* series is (see discussion guides above).

Specifically, Sarah was watching episode 5: 'Spirits of the ice forest'. She refers to the hatching of *Leaellynasaura* dinosaurs and the sequence takes place in the first 14 minutes, interspersed with some scenes of other dinosaurs.

The BBC seems to have taken down much of its online material on the series, though some remains at <http://www.bbc.co.uk/sn/prehistoric_life/tv_radio/wwdinosaurs/>. However, the ABC site still contains considerable online material on the series at <http://www.abc.net.au/dinosaurs/>, with a good outline of the science behind the making of Episode 5 at <http://www.abc.net.au/dinosaurs/chronology/106/makingof.htm>. You may also be able to get hold of *The making of walking with dinosaurs*, which has some interesting material on the decisions behind the program (some clips can be found on YouTube). Surprisingly, at the time the series was made, all that was known about the *Leaellynasaura* came from a single skull fossil. It would, of course, be possible to use the DVD directly, without reading and discussing the story first.

Walking with Dinosaurs worksheet

Part 1: Is that true?

Watch the DVD, concentrating on the scenes involving *Leaellynasaura*. As you watch the segment, fill in the table below by putting in examples from the DVD. How likely to be true do you think the 'facts' presented are? 'Facts' can be claims made by the narrator, or they may just be events depicted or visual evidence.

Include three examples in each column.

Category 1 <------------------------------ Most likely true	Category 2 ------------------------------ Possibly true	Category 3 ------------------------------> Least likely true
1. 2. 3.	1. 2. 3.	1. 2. 3.

Part 2: How do they know that?

In a pair, choose one of three 'facts' that each of you listed from each of the above columns.

Category 1: The 'fact' is ...

What sort of evidence do your think the makers of the documentary and their advisors would have had available to base their 'fact' on?	
What methods would they have used to gather this evidence, and to justify their inclusion of this 'fact'?	

Category 2: The 'fact' is …

What sort of evidence do your think the makers of the documentary and their advisors would have had available to base their 'fact' on?	
What methods would they have used to gather this evidence, and to justify their inclusion of this 'fact'?	

Category 3: The 'fact' is …

What sort of evidence do your think the makers of the documentary and their advisors would have had available to base their 'fact' on?	
What methods would they have used to gather this evidence, and to justify their inclusion of this 'fact'?	

Geological time

Geological time is so vast that it can be very difficult to get your head around it. Here's a practical exercise that can help students to see just how vast geological time is when compared to their own lifetimes.

Divide the class into small groups (perhaps three per group). Give each group a strip of narrow paper a little over 4.6 metres long – a roll of paper for a cash register is suitable. Also give them the table of events opposite.

Alternative: You could give them the table with no ages entered and ask them to find out how long ago each event happened. Since the dating of some of these events is controversial (e.g., when humans left Africa), this can raise some interesting issues. Students are also likely to find that the dates given for other events can vary somewhat in different sources, given that such dates are approximations.

Table of events

Event	Years ago
Earth first forms	4.6 billion
First life	4 billion
First multicellular life	1.5 billion
First complex life	530 million
First dinosaurs	230 million
Dinosaurs become extinct	65 million
First humans	2 million
Humans first leave Africa	100 000
First agriculture	10 000
Stonehenge discovered	3000
Birth of Christ	
European settlement of Australia (1788)	
Second World War starts	
Your first birthday	

Ask them to draw up a timeline using a true scale that shows all the events in the table above. It should be pretty obvious to them that they will need a scale of 1 metre = 1 billion years, but you can, of course, help them if they have any difficulty. First, they will need to mark the origin of the earth at one end of the tape, and the present day at the other. These marks ought to be 4.6 metres apart. Encourage them to start at the top and work towards the bottom of the table. Students will have to work out how many years ago the last four events were.

Of course, the task should be fairly easy at first, but it will become more difficult, and then impossible, as they get closer to the present. You can follow-up by asking them to:

1. Calculate the scaled distance there should be between the present and the last few dates given. This is good practice for the students in handling very small fractions! You may need to introduce some new metric units, like the micrometre and the nanometre.

2. Calculate how many years are shown by the width of the pencil line they have drawn for the present (if it is, say, 1 millimetre wide, it will cover one million years).

3. Ask them to choose a scale which would allow them to show the last few events clearly separated. A scale of 1 millimetre = 1 year might be suitable. Then get them to find out on a map how far their strip of paper would reach (on this scale, it will be 4600 kilometres long – that's further than Hobart to Darwin, or London to Cairo or New York to San Francisco).

Activity 9 | Lizards

"I went to visit my uncle up in Arnhem Land during the holidays," said Jenny. "I wrote an essay about him for Mrs Solomon. We had a lot of fun going out bush with him. He sure knows a lot!"

"What sort of stuff?" asked Alex.

"Well, all about lizards, goannas especially – what they eat, where they go at what times, how many there are – all that and more," she answered.

"How come he knows all that stuff? Is he a biologist?" queried Phong.

"No," laughed Jenny. "Partly it's because he hunts lizards, so he needs to watch them pretty carefully. But a lot is cultural knowledge, he told me, that he learned from the elders."

"I've got an aunt who studies lizards," Wai Ling interjected. "She goes bush too, for weeks at a time, looking for crowned geckos, way out near Broken Hill. They're endangered, so she's trying to find out all about them."

"Funny you should say that," responded Jenny. "My uncle has done some work with a lizard scientist called Pete – we talked to Pete and he said that he learns a whole lot more from Uncle Markum than he could from months of field trips."

"Maybe Aunt Jishen should do that too – save herself a lot of work."

"But your uncle just wants to catch the goannas to eat, Jenny," Phong interjected. "Scientists want all the facts, not just a meal. Science is about pure knowledge. How can your uncle's knowledge help that lizard scientist?"

"If you want a goanna meal out there, you had better know a few facts," Jenny hotly asserted, "because it's pretty rough country. And if you want to even see one lizard, let alone study it, those facts will help."

$\longrightarrow$

"So he's a sort of scientist," pondered Alex. "Anyhow, I don't think that scientists are just interested in pure knowledge. Wai Ling's aunt is trying to save those geckos, not just learn about them."

"Yeah," added Wai Ling, "I reckon anyone who is curious about the world – whether they want to use that knowledge or not – is a scientist."

"Yeah, well, I'm still not sure," Phong said. "Knowing facts is part of science, for sure, but don't scientists want more? Like explanations?"

Discussion guides

Jenny tells us that Uncle Markum has a good deal of scientific knowledge, and that she wrote an essay about it. Your students might be interested in hearing some of the details of such knowledge. If so, you might like to share Jenny's essay with them.

What I did in my holidays

During the holidays, I went to Arnhem Land to meet Uncle Markum, my father's brother. When Dad came south to get an education, Uncle Markum stayed. He told me he got an education too – not like Dad's, but just as tough. I can believe it: he sure knows a lot.

Here's an example. One day, we were driving along in his old Toyota ute when he shouted "Bungarra!" and pulled over. He ran to the edge of the long grass and peered at the ground. I was puzzled, but soon he came back with a goanna – that's what he meant by 'Bungarra'. He told me that he had to look for the fresh footprints, not in the sand, but among the stony gravel, because there he could get a more accurate indication of the goanna's speed, direction of travel and how long it had been since the goanna was there. He said that when the goanna moves the stones, you can see dampness or roughness underneath because these stones have been in the ground, rather than exposed to dust and wind.

He told me that we would have to prepare the goanna for eating later. He knew it was a female, but said that, as it is out of the breeding season, we could be sure there wouldn't be any eggs. I didn't help much, but later I watched him slit the goanna from neck to crutch underneath, and carefully open it up without disturbing the organs. He was looking for the sinews, buried deep in the goanna's body, which he carefully pulled out – otherwise the goanna would shrink up in the coals. After that, he could pull out the organs and put them aside for the old people. They always get the most nutritious bits, he told me.

It's a good hunting time, he added, just then at the beginning of the 'knock-'em-down' rain season. The goannas have plenty of flesh after the natural feed available over the previous three months. They are easier to catch too as it is getting cooler, and the animals are all getting sluggish.

I learnt so much from Uncle Markum – stuff I would never learn in school.

Many societies gather a huge amount of knowledge about the natural world. Hunters need to know about the habits of the animals they hunt and agriculturalists learn about how to grow plants successfully and to counteract pests; a need for accurate information about the seasons leads to detailed astronomical knowledge, and so on. To what extent is this knowledge science?

Jenny is clearly right when she says that people with other forms of knowledge can help scientists in their work. A biologist studying lizards, for example, can obviously learn from an Aboriginal hunter who knows the habits and behaviour of lizards. Such knowledge is built up over a great period of time. Scientists may only be able to do fieldwork for relatively short periods of time. Even if, for example, scientists had a year and were able to observe lizards in all four seasons, their observations would be limited. They would know about how the lizards behaved in that year, but not what differences there might be in wetter, drier, warmer or cooler seasons. Though a scientist could build up similar knowledge through many years of fieldwork, cultural knowledge can save the researcher a great deal of work and time.

However, Phong points out that the cultural context of hunter-gatherer knowledge may not be the same as the scientist's. A hunter might place more importance on certain groups of facts about lizards that assist in catching them. A scientist may be much more interested in their social relations, or their reproductive habits.

Is it possible that cultural knowledge contains insights that scientists, with their own objectives, miss? This is a question that can't be answered in a classroom discussion, though the possibility could be raised. Whether elements of modern science are different from most cultural knowledge forms is the core of the next issue.

1. Wai Ling's Aunt Jishen knows a lot about crowned geckos. Is she a scientist?
2. Jenny's Uncle Markum knows a lot about goannas. Is he a scientist?
3. Why do you think Uncle Markum's knowledge would be useful to Pete?
4. What are some of the similarities between the knowledge that Uncle Markum has, and the scientific knowledge that Pete wants?
5. What are some of the differences between the knowledge that Uncle Markum has, and the scientific knowledge that Pete wants?
6. Phong thinks that Uncle Markum and Pete have different aims, and this means that Uncle Markum's knowledge isn't science. Do you agree?
7. Do you think that anyone who has a lot of knowledge about the natural world is a scientist?
8. Is science just a western way of thinking about the world, or do all cultures have their own versions of science?

Observation, description and explanation

Phong wonders whether in order to do science, we have to go beyond observation and description to explanation. He is implying that while scientific cultural knowledge may be good at observing the natural world and describing what we see, this knowledge does not go on to develop western scientific explanations.

Observation involves looking carefully at the natural world to find out in detail how it appears to us. Description then records the results of those observations. Descriptions can take many forms: writing, storytelling, drawings and measurements.

Explanation goes beyond observation and description. It is quite possible to describe the world accurately even though the explanation for that description is entirely wrong. For example, lightning was explained by the ancient Greeks as a thunderbolt that the god Zeus had thrown, but this did not stop them from describing the appearance and effects of lightning accurately.

Explanation is a major goal of science, and it often invokes causes that are not observable (see discussion guides in Activities for 1: Magic, 2: Seeing Things, and

3: Unnatural Dangers). However, Zeus is not observable either, so there must be more to scientific explanation than invoking unobservable entities.

So, perhaps Phong is partly wrong in his comment. Older forms of knowledge often include explanations. However, he might be right in that the type of explanation offered is different to scientific explanations.

Science is dominated by mechanistic explanations. Philosophers argue about the exact nature of scientific explanation, but the following is one influential view which is quite accessible to school students: to explain some observation is to give an account of how it was caused, in terms of the mechanical interaction of entities with no will or thoughts of their own, such as particles and forces.

It is certainly arguable that, in physics and chemistry, such mechanistic explanation is central. But is it true in biology? As biology covers a wide range of studies, perhaps it depends on the branch of biology. Increasingly, biological studies involve biophysics and (especially) biochemistry – particularly when concerned with processes happening within an organism. In these areas, causal explanation is important.

Nevertheless, there are fields in biology where causal explanation seems to be less central. Ecological research relies on good, accurate observation and description of plants and animals and their interactions, while mechanistic explanation is hard to come by. Taxonomy – the classification of organisms – is also a field that depends more on describing anatomical and genetic similarities and differences than on finding mechanisms.

These considerations may lead us to conclude that valuable scientific work can be done in biology solely through detailed and accurate observation and description of animals, plants and the communities they form, as we see with Uncle Markum's knowledge.

Before you lead your students into a discussion on these topics, you might like to expose them to some simple examples of both mythological explanation through traditional stories and scientific explanation of the habits of some animals. (e.g., Blackrose 2011)

1. Phong wonders about the need for explanations in science. Do you think that Uncle Markum's knowledge about goannas includes explanations?

2. Do you think that scientific knowledge, like Aunt Jishen's about crowned geckos, includes explanations?
3. Does scientific knowledge about the habits of a lizard have to include an explanation?
4. What sort of explanation counts as a scientific explanation?

Activity 10 | Experiments

"I'm confused," complained Andy as the children left their science classroom at the end of the day.

"You're not the only one," wailed Emma. A group of them walked slowly towards the front gate of the school grounds.

"Mr Carey throws so many ideas at us that I never get time to swallow them all." Maeve kicked a pebble as she walked.

"Yeah, experiments!" Andy said with feeling. "All those things we have to remember. I don't know how scientists ever prove anything."

"That's easy." Luigi always seemed to think everything was easy. "They just look at things often enough and then they know. Like, the sun comes up every morning, and they see it, so then they know that the sun will come up every morning in the future."

"Just like you've always known the answer to everything in the past, so you're always gonna know all the answers," muttered Maeve.

"That's a bit unfair. It's not right to mock people," Emma cut in.

"And it's not right to say that just because something has always happened in the past, it always will," said Alex. "Like, my mum always cuts my sandwiches, but I'll bet she won't always cut them."

"Yeah, you're right," Luigi mused. "It's not just seeing something happen again and again. But it does work sometimes, doesn't it? Like with the sun."

"So why does it work sometimes and not others?" asked Jenny. "Is there a rule?"

"I reckon it's got something to do with that fair test stuff," put in Andy. "If we do a fair test, then we *have* to know the answer, don't we?"

$\longrightarrow$

"I don't know about that." Emma was looking puzzled. "We say we've made the two things the same in every way, but how do we know that there isn't …" A football being kicked around by some bigger boys landed in the middle of their group, causing Alex to drop his books and everyone to jump.

By the time they were walking together again, Maeve had another question. "How do these scientists get to do experiments, anyway?" she asked.

"That's easy," answered Luigi. "They just go out and set up a fair test. You just do the experiment to find out the answer."

"But where do they come from?" persisted Maeve. "All the experiments we do are given to us by Mr Carey. Who gives the scientists their experiments?"

"They would have to dream them up themselves," said Emma.

"Dream?" laughed Alex. "You're not telling me they get them in their dreams?"

"No, of course not, silly," smiled Emma, good-naturedly. "I mean they *think* them up for themselves."

"But a thought can't just pop up out of nowhere," Maeve persevered. "Where do these thoughts come from?"

"I don't know. Some of my thoughts seem to come from nowhere," said Andy. "But," he conceded, "Plenty don't. Most of them come out of stuff I'm already thinking."

"That's got to be it," Jenny asserted. "These scientists have a …" Just then the sound of a car's horn cut across their conversation. Jenny's mother was waving frantically at her from across the road.

"Oh, I've got to run," she exclaimed. "Mum needs to go into town today and she told me not to be late!" As she dashed off, most of the others noticed the buses had begun loading and wandered off too.

Emma was left standing with Alex. "Well, we didn't decide much. I have just about as many questions now as I started out with," she said.

"Is that all?" Alex asked with a twinkle in his eye. "I reckon I've got ten times more questions. I was confused after that class, but now there seems to be even more to doing experiments than I thought."

Discussion guides

Induction

Inductive reasoning is reasoning from a number of particular instances to a generalisation. Luigi gives a famous example: the sun coming up in the morning. (If you discuss this example, some students are likely to point out that the sun doesn't rise – the earth turns. However, the point about induction nevertheless still holds.)

As Alex points out, lots of examples do not entail that the generalisation is true. A famous historical example is the claim, quite convincing in Europe some centuries ago, that all swans are white. The discovery of black swans in Australia showed that a strongly supported inductive generalisation was false (see counter examples in the discussion guides for Activity 12: Bouncing Balls).

The problem of induction begs the question: how many examples are needed to give certainty to the generalisation? The answer, strictly speaking, is that no number is sufficient (unless there are a finite number of cases, and you have seen them all). Yet we trust inductive generalisations all the time, often with no problems. It seems that the number of examples we need to examine, in order to draw a reliable conclusion, depends on many factors including the nature of the case we are looking at and our knowledge of the background to the case.

1. Is Luigi right that the sun will rise tomorrow? Why?
2. Is Alex right that his mother will not always make his sandwiches? Why?
3. If you open a packet of identical biscuits you have never tasted before, and you don't like the first one, how many biscuits do you have to try before you decide whether you won't like any of them?
4. If you meet a person from another country and they are happy, can you conclude that all people from that country are happy? How many happy people from that country would you have to meet to draw that conclusion?
5. Walking down the street, you meet five different dogs, one after the other, and each of them wags its tail. How sure can you be that the next dog will wag its tail when it meets you?
6. How many times do you have to see something happening the same way before you can be sure the next time it happens it will be the same?

7. What sorts of factors influence how sure you can be that things will keep happening the same way they did in the past?
8. How much do you believe that things will keep happening in the same way in your everyday life?

Induction and science

A simple view of science is the one taken by Luigi: scientists look to see whether things happen in the same way repeatedly. If they do, scientists say they have discovered a law – this thing will always happen the same way. Certainly, scientific laws are general statements: they claim that all relevantly similar events will happen in the same way. For example, Newton's Law of Universal Gravitation: any two masses will always attract with a force that depends on their respective masses and distance apart.

Certainly, the observation that certain events seem to happen according to a pattern has to be a part of what a scientist does. Yet the problem of induction means we cannot be sure that future events will happen just as past events have, especially if we have been looking at the events under a particular set of conditions. For this reason, repeated experiments or observations, while they can give more confidence, cannot prove a scientific law. Yet a single contrary example can show that the generalisation is unsound (such as finding a black swan in Australia). Hence, scientists are often guided by looking for contrary examples, under novel conditions, in order to test their theories. While passing the new test gives some further credence to their theory (how much?), it never proves it. The theory can be falsified by a contrary result, leading to refinement or even abandonment of the theory (see also section on Hypothesis on p. 84).

Of course, we informally test our everyday theories in a similar way, even if we are not systematic about it.

1. Try holding a pen in the air and letting go. Does it fall? Can you conclude that all pens will fall if they are dropped?
2. You go on holiday to a new place for two weeks. It rains every day. Can you conclude that it always rains there every day?
3. How would you test your theory about falling pens?
4. How would you test your theory about rainy days?
5. Does repeatedly testing your theory prove that it is right?

6. Does repeatedly testing your theory in lots of different ways prove that it is right?

7. If you keep testing your theory, and one of your tests doesn't work, does that show your theory is wrong? Are there any other possibilities?

Doing an experiment

Scientists will often talk about true experiments as opposed to quasi-experiments – especially in the social sciences, where situations can be very complex. In this sense, a *true* experiment is one in which all the variables are tightly controlled – what is often called a *fair test* in science classes. Only in true experiments can we demonstrate that the input variable causes the output variable.

Yet, many other situations can be considered experiments in a wider sense. If a child pours water on an anthill, just to see what happens, we say they are experimenting, yet no other variables are being controlled. Would we still say they are experimenting if they were watching intently as water just happened to flow into an anthill for some other reason?

The purpose of the discussion guide below is to get your students to think more carefully about what features can be included in experiments to make them more reliable, taking into account the purpose of an experiment. Finally, they might consider how experiments are planned.

1. If you watch something happen, is that an experiment?
2. If you make something happen and then watch it, is that an experiment?
3. If you make something happen and watch it, then try to figure out why it happened, is that an experiment?
4. If you plan to make something happen in a special way, with the idea of finding out about how it happens, is that an experiment?
5. What are the differences between an experiment and just doing something?
6. What features make experiments better, so that you can be certain that you can believe you understand what's happening and why?
7. Why do scientists do experiments?
8. Where do the plans that scientists have for experiments come from?

Hypothesis

When we set students to do an experiment in their science class, and we ask them to write up a standard scientific report, one of the first headings we use is 'Hypothesis'. The common answer that is given if students want to know what 'hypothesis' means is that it is an educated guess. Often, for experiments that a teacher has told you to do, this is what it turns out to be.

Yet for a scientist who is working at the cutting edge of science, things are somewhat different. Unlike the student, who is merely following instructions, the scientist is working through a problem that matters to them, and they have a theory about it. On the basis of this theory, they work out what ought to happen: this is their hypothesis. The experiment is aimed at testing whether their theory is adequate, in the sense that it will predict accurately what will happen in specified circumstances. Is this an educated guess? Well, it is certainly educated, but it isn't a guess – rather, it is entailed by their theory. Since the theory entails the hypothesis, then a failure of the experiment to work out that way implies that there is something wrong: either the theory is wrong, or the experiment is flawed.

Of course, scientists can also set up situations where they try something just to see what happens. This approach is used when there is no settled theory, when the scientist is 'playing around', trying to get a sense of the field. These are not 'true experiments' and it makes no sense to say that they have a hypothesis. They may have an educated guess in mind, if they have the inklings of a possible theory, or it may be pure trial and error.

Many school science experiments are like this, at least as far as the students are concerned. If students do not have at least an implicit theory about the area, then it makes little sense to ask them for a hypothesis. If it is to really be a hypothesis, then they should be able to explain why they think the outcome they predict will happen, on the basis of some understanding of the situation.

1. Why do you think scientists conduct an experiment? Is it to see what will happen? It is to check their ideas about what should happen? Is it to prove a theory?
2. If scientists know in advance what is going to happen in their experiment, is this cheating?

3. If scientists know in advance what is going to happen in their experiment, why do they bother doing them?
4. Which tells scientists more: an experiment that works the way they thought it would, or one that doesn't work the way they thought it would?
5. What do scientists do when an experiment doesn't work the way they thought it would?
6. What are the similarities and differences between a hypothesis and a guess, a hunch, an educated guess and/or a prediction?

When is a 'fair test' fair?

When designing an experiment, the experimental (input and output) variables can be pretty obvious. So can some of the variables that need to be controlled. However, there are many possible factors that can vary between two different tests in an experiment, and we cannot keep them all the same. (If we do them at the same time, they must be in different places – if in the same place, they must be at different times.) Nor do we need to. Most of these variables will make no difference to the outcome of the experiment.

So, we need to control all, and only those other variables which would have an effect on the outcome. How do we know, in advance of our experiments, which variables will need to be controlled? We don't – we have to make a guess – usually an educated one. If we don't control a variable which turns out to have an effect on the experiment, we can get misleading results.

In school science, the variables to consider are often given to students. Cutting edge scientists don't have that luxury. Failing to realise that a particular variable had to be controlled has led to some false conclusions. A famous example is the horse that could do arithmetic, Clever Hans. Repeated tests seemed to show that the horse could, for example, add two numbers and stamp his hoof the right number of times. It was only when psychologist Oskar Pfungst (1911) thought to make sure the questioner was not in the horse's field of view that the truth came out: Hans was responding to unintended body language.

Working out which variables need controlling is a mixture of scientific knowledge and imagination.

1. What is a fair test?
2. Why is a fair test fair?

3. Think of an experiment you have done. Was it a fair test? Why?
4. Would it matter if you did the different tests in rooms at different temperatures?
5. Would it matter if you did the different tests at different times of day?
6. Would it matter if you did the different tests on different parts of the desk?
7. Would it matter if you did the different tests using different equipment?
8. Would it matter if you did the different tests wearing different clothes?
9. How can we tell which things *must* be the same in a fair test?

Activity 11 | Animals

Emma was in a fighting mood. "Look at this article," she fumed, waving a scrap of newspaper in the air. "They take poor little mice and they deliberately give them cancer, just so they can test out some new drugs!"

"I bet if you get that cancer, you won't be so angry about those tests on those mice. Maybe that drug will be just the one to cure you," countered Luigi. "How else are they going to know?"

"Huh. Why don't they test it in some other way, like in a test tube or something," replied Emma. "Or maybe on humans – they can say whether they agree to it or not, unlike those poor little mice."

"Well," Jenny put in, "I think they do all those things before the drug gets sold. They wouldn't use it on mice if they didn't think it might work, would they? And then they wouldn't give it to humans, if they hadn't checked with mice that it doesn't do something else nasty."

"So the nasty stuff happens to mice, hey?" asked Andy. "Emma's right – the mice don't get asked if they want to take that risk."

"Asking a mouse for permission?" laughed Luigi. "They can't do that – mice just aren't smart enough. They …"

"Whether they're smart or not has nothing to do with it!" interjected Emma. "They can suffer, can't they? And it's wrong if any animal gets hurt."

"Yeah, right … Better lock up cats and feed them on porridge instead of mice," muttered Jenny, but Emma and Andy ignored her.

"True," admitted Luigi, "suffering isn't good. But if the scientists don't do experiments on those mice, then a lot of humans with cancer are going to suffer. And we're much more important than mice. All mice can do is sniff around after cheese, but humans can do so much more."

$\longrightarrow$

"Yeah, well, human suffering is as important as mice's suffering," conceded Andy, "but I don't think it's any more important. If more mice than humans suffer, or if there are other ways to test drugs, then we shouldn't be testing on mice."

"There can't be other ways, can there?" asked Jenny. "Otherwise scientists would be using them. Anyway, who says that what works on mice will work on humans?"

"Maybe, maybe – that's if they can be bothered to look for other ways," said Emma. "I bet they don't."

"I wouldn't know – maybe, maybe not," admitted Luigi. "But surely it's important to find out more about cancer and cancer drugs. A few mice that can't feel very much anyway aren't as important, are they? What if it was a choice between your pet mouse dying and your mum getting an incurable cancer? Which would you choose?"

Emma and Andy were speechless for a moment. "We'd choose our mums, of course," Emma finally asserted. "But is the choice as black and white as that?"

Discussion guides

Discussing versus debating

A common way of dealing with ethical issues such as this is to stage a debate, with the students allocated to being 'for' or 'against' animal testing. Debates can be engaging and invigorating, but they pose one great danger: they imply that such issues are black and white. In reality, an issue such as animal testing is complex, and it is quite possible to take middle ground. There are many positions between an outright ban of any use of animals in science, and an approach which is completely open slather.

In a discussion in a community of inquiry, 'for' and 'against' sides can develop, and so the discussion can resemble a debate. However, a community of inquiry can also bring out a number of different views, so that the discussion becomes much more nuanced. Further, the participants have not been signed up to defend one side at all costs, and to seek only the negative in another view.

Hence, they are free to modify, or even abandon, their view in the light of good reasons for doing so.

As the facilitator of the community, you can encourage students to seek agreement where possible, to acknowledge the strength of objections that others raise to the point they have made, and to seek out important distinctions, or exceptions to the opinions advanced in the discussion.

Using animals in research

Students might be tempted to condemn all animal research after reading this story, before they consider the full range of research that involves animals. Experiments can differ in many ways: how much (if at all) they involve animal suffering, the importance of research outcomes (from testing cosmetics to finding cures for diseases), and in the intended beneficiaries of the research (humans, others of their species, the animal itself).

1. Is it morally permissible to do an experiment, using an animal, if the animal is not harmed at all?
2. Is it morally permissible to do an experiment on an animal that causes little harm, but it will recover?
3. Is it morally permissible to do an experiment on an animal that harms it a lot, but it will recover?
4. Is it morally permissible to do an experiment on an animal that harms it a lot and it will never recover?
5. Would it change any of your answers to the above four questions if the experiment would save many people some discomfort?
6. Would it change any of your answers to the first four questions if the experiment promised to lead to an important breakthrough that would save many people's lives?
7. Would it change any of your answers to the first four questions if the experiment promised to lead to an important breakthrough that would save the lives of many other animals?
8. Would it be morally permissible to experiment on an animal if it might save that animal's own life?
9. Under what circumstances, if any, do you think it would be OK to experiment on an animal?

10. Under what circumstances do you think it would be morally acceptable to experiment on humans?

Informed consent

Before using human subjects in experiments, researchers have to obtain informed consent. They must explain the experiment, its aims, and the possible dangers of taking part. However, some problems can arise. What should the participants be told, and in how much detail? In some cases, knowing the intent of the experiment may distort the results. In your discussion, the related issue that doctors are generally required to obtain informed consent before treating a patient, may also come up.

Clearly, obtaining informed consent is not possible with animals. We can take one of two attitudes here: the animals' inability to understand anything about the experiment means we can experiment on them as we choose, or that this inability implies it would be unfair to subject them to something they cannot understand.

1. If I wanted to experiment on you, should I have to tell you what I am going to do? Why?
2. If I wanted to experiment on you, should I have to get your permission first? Why?
3. How much should I have to tell you about the experiment, when I ask your permission? What sorts of things should I tell you?
4. If you don't, or can't, give your permission, does that mean I would be morally wrong to go ahead with the experiment?
5. Can a mouse give permission to have an experiment done on it?
6. If a mouse can't give permission, does that mean that we should not do experiments on mice?
7. If a doctor is going to treat you, should they make sure you understand the treatment and its possible side effects, before they go ahead?
8. If we cannot experiment on an animal because it can't give its consent, does this mean a vet shouldn't treat a sick animal for the same reason?

Utilitarianism

One of the major ethical theories used in arguments about animal experimentation is utilitarianism. Put simply, it says that the morally right action is the one that leads to the greatest balance of happiness and pleasure over pain and suffering. (Note that this is the sum total, not any one individual's, happiness and suffering.) Several prominent utilitarian philosophers, including Australia's Peter Singer, author of *Animal liberation* (1975), point out that the pleasures and suffering of animals should be counted, as well as those of human beings.

Such arguments are used by many who oppose animal experimentation on moral grounds; but it should be noted that a utilitarian argument for animal experimentation can also be used, if it could be shown that the gain for humans outweighs the suffering of the animals.

Utilitarianism assumes that all things morally good amount to increased happiness or pleasure, and all things morally bad equate to pain and suffering. This can be questioned: maybe there are some things which are morally valuable independent of pleasure and pain. One possibility is that humans and animals have an intrinsic worth (see section on Intrinsic worth below).

Utilitarian calculation

1. Is it a bad thing that the mice suffer?
2. Is it a bad thing when humans suffer?
3. Is suffering the only bad thing there is? Are all other bad things just different types of suffering?
4. Does a mouse's suffering count the same as human suffering?
5. Is it always good to feel pleasure?
6. Is pleasure/happiness the only good thing there is? Are all other good things just different types of pleasure?
7. If the only way to get humans to feel pleasure (e.g., by being cured of cancer) is for a lot of mice to suffer (by being experimental animals), does that make using the mice morally OK?
8. If the amount of suffering the mice experience is greater than the amount of pleasure the humans get, does that make using the mice morally bad?

9. Is all that matters, morally, in any situation just whether there is more suffering or more pleasure created?
10. Are there some things that are morally bad, even if they create more happiness than suffering? Are there some things that are morally good, even if they create more suffering than happiness?

Another way to question utilitarianism is to look at some of the implications of accepting it, and to see that they seem absurd. In implying that we should turn cats into vegetarians so they won't catch and kill mice, Jenny raises such an objection: that utilitarianism applied to animals seems to imply that we are morally obliged to lessen suffering by stopping predators catching prey.

Utilitarianism and predation

1. If it is a bad thing that mice suffer, does that mean we should always try to stop them suffering?
2. If we should, then should we save a mouse if we see a cat is about to catch it?
3. If a cat already has a mouse, but hasn't killed or badly injured it yet, should we try to save the mouse?
4. Should we always try to save an animal from future suffering, if we can?
5. If so, does this mean we should put all predators in zoos, and feed them animals that have already died naturally?
6. If it is morally OK to allow predators to kill prey, is that compatible with saying all suffering is bad?
7. If it is morally OK to allow predators to kill prey, then why isn't it equally OK for humans to cause suffering of other animals, for our own good?

Intrinsic worth

Some ethical theories that oppose utilitarianism claim that humans have an intrinsic moral worth, and rights that go with that worth (e.g., Kant 1998). Versions of these theories can extend the notion of rights and intrinsic worth to animals as well (Regan 1985). Such rights mean that we cannot act morally if we violate those rights, even if the action would lead to greater happiness overall.

Animal rights theories usually claim that an animal has a right to live its own life, without our interference. Each animal is valuable in itself, not merely because we value it. This raises an interesting question: What is the origin of this intrinsic value? It is easy to see how value arises when somebody values a thing for its usefulness. My pet dog is valuable because I love him. But where does intrinsic value come from? Some say from God, or from life itself.

However, even granted that animals have a worth of their own, it can be questioned, as Luigi does, whether that value is equal for all animals (including humans), or whether some animals are worth more than others. If they are, we can ask, what makes them more valuable?

1. If you have a pet, is your pet's existence valuable to you? Why?
2. Is your pet's existence as valuable to you as your parents' existence? If yes, why? If not, then why not?
3. Is your pet as valuable as a wild animal that has never been known by humans?
4. Is your pet as valuable as a human you have never met?
5. If you, and anyone else who cares for your pet, were all to disappear from the pet's life, would the pet's existence still have value? What sort of value?
6. If there had never been any humans, would animals still have value? How?
7. Is it possible for an animal to have value without someone to value it? Does value require a valuer?

Follow-up activity

The discussion that arises from this story would be good preparation for a research project, perhaps requiring students to write a position paper: a short essay stating the position that they take on the issue, their supporting reasons, and a summary of how they deal with the arguments that might disagree with the position they take.

In looking further into the issue, students should be encouraged to find a variety of sources. If they are using the internet – which is probably the easiest source – they should either try to find sites that give a balanced account (such as the first below), or find several reputable sites which come from opposite sides (such as the last two below). It is also important to encourage students to make a judgement about how reliable these sites are.

Websites:

Animal Experimentation: International Debate Education Association

http://www.idebate.org/debatabase/topic_details.php?topicID=7

Australian and New Zealand Council for the Care of Animals in Research & Teaching

http://www.adelaide.edu.au/ANZCCART/humane/benefit.html

Animals Australia

http://www.animalsaustralia.org/issues/animal_experimentation.php

Activity 12 | Bouncing Balls

The children raced out the door – it was break time. Some went off to sit and talk, others went to look at the pond. Emma joined the 'sporty' group – she wanted to talk them into playing hockey today. As she approached, she could hear them already arguing about which game to play.

"Why can't we play hockey?" she demanded. "I've brought my hockey ball and stick and we haven't played for ages."

"You might have your stick," said Tom, "but we haven't all got one."

"That's a good reason," Emma had to concede. "I know! Let's play the game that we can think of the best reason for."

But this didn't seem to be much help. Those who had a ball – Andy had a soccer ball, Sarah, a netball, Alex, a cricket ball and bat and Jenny, a tennis ball to play handball – claimed their game was best and wouldn't admit that anyone else had a better reason than theirs. "We'll never agree," wailed Luigi. "What other reason can we think of?"

"Well, let's play the game that uses the best ball – that's got to be the ball that bounces the highest," said Emma. Alex looked disgusted and muttered something about not thinking that was a very good reason, but the others shouted their agreement.

"That's easy," said Sarah. "This will bounce highest," and she demonstrated by flipping the netball up onto the grass so that it bounced back to her hand.

"Huh," sneered Andy, showing that the soccer ball would also bounce back to his hand. Jenny did likewise with her tennis ball, adding that she didn't see that Sarah's bounce proved anything much about which ball was best, but at least it ruled out playing cricket.

"Oh, yeah?" Alex stepped onto the concrete path and hurled the cricket ball at the concrete – it bounced higher than any of the others had.

$\longrightarrow$

"I can make this bounce higher, though." Sarah flung the netball at the soft grassy ground, and, sure enough, it bounced higher, "and that was on the grass, not on the concrete!"

"The soccer ball will bounce highest of all!" Andy ran into the classroom block and belted up the stairs.

"Let's get out of here," whispered Alex to Emma, "this is getting silly." As they walked away a figure appeared at the third-floor window and a soccer ball hurtled down, bounced on the concrete and high into the air. From around the corner, Mrs Sharkey appeared, shouting at Andy to come down at once, while the others scattered.

"There goes Andy's chance of playing soccer today," commented Alex. "I still wonder which ball would have bounced best, though. How could we have worked it out?"

"That's easy – we just needed to test them properly, without all that showing off. What I'm wondering is why *do* balls bounce at all?"

"It's because of the air in them," said Alex. He seemed pretty sure of himself.

"Well, what about the cricket ball? It doesn't bounce much, but it still bounces, especially when you smash it into the ground like you did. And it doesn't have air in it. Nor does one of those bouncy balls, you know, the little solid rubber ones."

Alex had to agree with Emma on this. "That's true. But I think you'd have to look very closely at what happens when the ball hits the ground, 'cos that's when it bounces."

"Yeah, but it all happens so fast – how could you see it?" Emma frowned.

"High-speed photography."

"OK, but that hasn't been around forever. I bet they knew how balls bounced before all that. But how did they work it out?" asked Emma.

"I guess they did … and the explanation must work for all balls, I reckon. They all bounce pretty much the same, whether they're made of leather or rubber, whether they're full of air or solid. So what happens when they bounce must be pretty much the same too."

Discussion guides

The fair test – variables and their relationships

This story raises a number of ideas that lie at the heart of scientific endeavour. Moreover, it introduces a number of issues which have a much wider input than science, but which play central roles in scientific inquiry: issues of curiosity and puzzlement, and the sort of thinking on which scientists and many others rely.

The most central idea here, at least as far as the experimental sciences go, is the idea of a fair test. This is quite a complex idea for those new to it. Grasping it depends on having a clear idea of what we mean by 'variables', distinguishing them from values (or measurements), and knowing what we mean by a relationship between two variables.

A variable is a property which may be described or measured, and which may take different values. For example, some of the variables in Bouncing Balls were the type of ball, the surface on which it bounced (these variables can be described), the height from which the ball is dropped, the height to which it bounces, or the force with which it is thrown (these are all variables which can be measured).

Each variable will have several, or many, values. The type of ball can be a cricket ball, netball, hockey ball and so on. The height it is dropped from can take any value – 1 metre, 10 metres and so on.

When the value of one variable is linked in some way to the value of another, we say there is a relationship between the values of these two variables. The relationship may be descriptive, for example, when the type of ball is related to the height to which it will bounce. The relationship may also be mathematical, for example, when the height from which the ball is dropped is related to the height to which it bounces. In order to test whether there truly is a relationship between two variables, the values of all the other variables need to be the same (i.e., they are controlled).

In any experiment, there will be three types of variables. There is the one that the experimenter is deliberately changing (which can be called the input or independent variable). There is the one that the experimenter thinks is related to the input variable, and will be measuring each time a trial is done (the output or dependent variable). Finally, all other variables the experimenter thinks might also affect the output variable have to be controlled each time a trial is done. If one variable is changed between trials, then any difference we see in the value of the output variable might be due to that, and not to the change in the value of the input variable.

Here's an example. Your students might wonder which type of ball will bounce highest. They are predicting a relationship between the input variable 'type of ball' and the output variable 'height of bounce'. In order to test this properly, they will need to ensure that each time they change the type of ball (test a new value of the input variable) all other factors that might affect how high the ball bounces must be kept the same. Before they can do this, they need to brainstorm everything that they think might affect the bounce. It isn't always obvious what variables might alter the outcome and hence need to be controlled.

1. Why weren't the kids in the story able to work out which ball bounced best?
2. What things do you think might make a difference to the height a ball will bounce?
3. Are any of the variables we have mentioned related to each other? In what way are they related? Why do you think so?
4. How could we find out if any of these ideas are right?
5. If we are testing balls to find out which one will bounce best, how should we go about it?
6. How can we be sure that the variable we think is making the difference to how high the ball bounces is the right one, rather than another variable?
7. If we are changing just one thing (say, the type of ball) and keeping all the rest of the variables the same, can we be sure that the ball that bounces highest under those conditions will always bounce higher under a different set of controlled conditions (say, on a different surface)? How could we test?
8. What makes a test fair?

Visualisation

Students can often think that science is all about observation and rationality. However, other ways of thinking are often important. In the case of working out why a ball bounces, Alex is right to suggest that we can see what's going on if we use high-speed photography, but Emma is also right to point out other ways. In particular, scientists often have to use their imagination to visualise processes that are, for some reason, difficult or impossible to observe directly.

In discussion (especially question 3 below), students may well be able to work out what happens, and why it helps explain bouncing. Some small demonstrations can also help – students might suggest some, or you might. It is likely that (maybe with a little general direction from you) students will realise the ball squashes on impact, and that in returning to its original shape, it pushes itself off the ground. They may take this further in realising the ground does something similar. To demonstrate the former, a tennis ball can be pressed down on a desk, then released (perhaps it is best to press it down touching the sides rather than the top). The latter can be demonstrated by laying a springy ruler across a gap between two books, and pressing an object onto it so it bends and then releasing it.

1. Why can't you see what really happens when a ball bounces?
2. How could people tell what happened when a ball bounced before high-speed photography?
3. What do you think (in your mind's eye) happens to the ball and to the ground when a ball bounces?
4. Are there any other examples of events that scientists might want to explain that they would have trouble in observing properly? What's the problem?
5. Are there any alternative ways of trying to figure out what happens, apart from looking closely at it?
6. Are there any problems with trying to imagine (in your mind's eye) what goes on when it is too fast/tiny/huge/far away/long ago to observe directly?
7. How can you check that the process you visualise is a good explanation?

Idealisation

Scientists are not so much interested in explaining one particular incident, as in finding general explanations for whole classes of incidents. They don't want to know how the tennis ball bounces, but how all balls bounce. Note that this is different from, say, how historians approach knowledge. They are often looking primarily for a way to explain this particular incident in history – maybe the origin of the first Gulf War – and only then might they consider how that explanation works for wars in general.

In generalising, a scientist will ignore properties that are not considered essential to the explanation, such as the colour of the ball, or the material it is made of. This means effectively that the scientist is considering an imaginary or idealised ball, which lacks features (like colour) that all real balls must have. In idealising, judgements have to be made about which properties do or don't make a difference. For example, colour is unlikely to make any difference to how a ball bounces, but the material it is made from, while not important in a general explanation, will most likely cause subtle differences in a more detailed explanation.

1. Do you think Alex is right when he says that the explanation must work for all balls, whether they are made of leather or rubber or have air or not? Why?
2. Why don't we try to work out an explanation of how a particular ball bounces, rather than an imaginary ball?
3. If you are trying to explain why a ball bounces, which features are unimportant? Which are important? Why?
4. How come we can ignore some features in working out an explanation?
5. Does this mean that our explanation only works for imaginary balls (which aren't made in any particular way)?
6. Would all balls behave exactly like the imaginary ball we use in our explanation?

Counter examples and falsification

When Alex advances an idea as to why balls bounce because of the air in them, Emma offers a counter example – the cricket ball. Finding a counter example is a powerful technique in critical thinking and holds a special place in scientific thought.

A counter example can be used to test universal claims that are meant to cover all cases of a certain sort. Scientific claims are like this. For this reason, philosopher of science Karl Popper (1959) asserted that science progresses, not just by finding new universal claims, but also by seeking to find counter examples. Scientific knowledge then consists of all those universal claims that have not yet been falsified by finding counter examples. For example, Einstein's Theory of Relativity replaced Newton's Laws when examples were found of situations (involving very high masses and/or velocities) which were exceptions to the latter.

While Popper's account has been challenged in detail, it does seem that his insight captures something of how science works. Many cases in which a scientific theory accounts for the evidence cannot prove it must be true, because a single inexplicable exception acts as a counter example, and thus reveals the theory is flawed.

1. Why did Emma say "Well, what about the cricket ball? … It doesn't have air in it."
2. Did Emma prove that it wasn't true that balls bounce because of the air in them?
3. How can one example prove something?
4. Does giving one example always prove something?
5. Can you give an example of where one example doesn't prove anything?
6. Can you give an example of where one example does prove something?
7. Under what conditions will a single example prove something?
8. Say we have a scientific theory about how something works, and use it to make a prediction of what will happen in an experiment. If the experiment happens in a way we didn't predict, what does this mean for our theory?

Criteria and operationalising variables

When we identify a variable, then it can be quite difficult to figure out how to measure it. The children in the story have this problem. Even if they decide to play the game that uses the best ball, the term 'best' is pretty vague. Emma quickly expands 'best' into 'bounces the highest'. But there are probably many other ways we might do so. Why not the prettiest, or the brightest, or the furriest? Why not a combination of these?

Emma has suggested a criterion for being the best ball. Under the right circumstances this criterion can be measured reasonably easily. She has 'operationalised' the variable 'best'. It is not so easy to see how one would measure the prettiest ball. Similarly, if a scientist decides that one of the variables is, say, hardness (of a geological mineral), or intelligence (of a person), then they will have to be able to find something they can measure which seems to be sufficiently like what they mean by hardness or intelligence. In the former case (i.e., hardness) this becomes whether the mineral will scratch, or be scratched by, other minerals. In the latter case (intelligence), the person's performance can be measured with an IQ test. But we can still ask whether these ways of operationalising those variables are good, or whether there might be better ways.

1. Is the ball that bounces highest, the best ball?
2. What other criteria for being the best ball could we have?
3. Would they all be equally easy to measure? How would you measure each of the criteria that have been suggested?
4. Might the best ball be one that meets a number of different criteria most adequately, rather than just one criterion?
5. If you were trying to make the best ball, what would you need to figure out before you started planning how to make it?
6. Can there be such a thing as a 'best ball'?
7. Could something be the best under some circumstances, but not in others?
8. If we can't always agree that one ball is better than another, does that mean all balls are equally good or equally bad?

Follow-up experiment

This relatively open-ended experiment will require students to identify the variables, as well as to carry out a controlled experiment (fair test). The discussion based on the story Bouncing Balls may well have addressed the question of identifying and controlling variables and, in this discussion, the class will most likely have identified most of the possible variables involved. If not, there might be a need to discuss such matters before setting this experiment.

Supply the students with multiple balls (a variety of different types) and some long rulers (metre rules).

You may need to help the students as they decide their research question. Remember, it ought to be one that can be answered by taking several values of only a single input variable, and that variable must be able to be measured using available equipment. This experiement is designed for small groups, so whether you require a report written cooperatively, or one from each student, is up to you. Students should be able to complete this work in 1.5 to 2 hours, maybe split over two sessions. The instructions you can give them are opposite.

Bouncing balls

Information: A ball dropped from a height onto a surface will bounce, but the height to which it bounces depends on a number of factors. Our discussion after the Bouncing Balls story covered much of the background information you need to do this investigation.

The task: You are to carry out a fair test investigation, in your group, into *only one* of the factors that affects the height to which a ball will bounce. You will need to:

- decide exactly what question you want to answer
- identify the likely factors that might affect the height a ball bounces
- draw up a list of the possible variables and decide which you will investigate and how. You need to consider the practicalities (time, equipment, making it a fair test, being able to measure or control your variables, etc) of setting up the experiment at this stage
- predict what the results will be
- carry out your tests and record the results
- evaluate your results and draw your conclusions.

The report: Using the following headings, write a report.

Title: . . . .

Question: What question are you going to answer? What are the important factors you will investigate? Be clear about your input variable, and which variables you will control.

Predictions: What do you think will happen *before* you do the tests? Why?

Method: Describe in detail what you will do.

Results: Present your results neatly, fully and carefully. You might want to use a table, though you need to state your findings in words.

Conclusion: Explain the different starting values of your input variable, and whether this is what you predicted. Discuss any difficulties or any specific factors which might have led to unreliable results. Finally, say what you consider to be the most likely explanation and why.

Activity 13 | Unnatural Dangers

"I read something really gross last night," said Greta, as she sat down with her friends Conchita and Phong in the school canteen to eat her lunch. "In the paper it said cheap ice-creams are made out of a chemical that's used in making shoe polish! Nasty unnatural chemicals – I don't want them in my food! And shoe polish – yuck! How could people eat that? It must be really bad for you. And how can those scientists even work out how to make such yucky stuff into food? They shouldn't even try to do things like that – it's just bad." She reached for the salt to put a bit more on her chips.

"Watch out!" shouted Conchita. "Don't put that salt on those chips!"

Greta blanched and snatched the salt shaker away from her chips. "Why not?" she asked.

"Because … you remember what we've learned in science, don't you? Salt is sodium chloride. You remember what happened when we chucked that sodium in water the other day …"

"Yeah, it was great!" snorted Phong. "It was all fizz and flames – especially when Luigi got Mr Carey to put that big piece in. It was almost an explosion!"

"But what's that got to do with my chips?" queried Greta. "Salt doesn't explode on my tongue. And I've heard you need salt to live. In history we were learning about how people who live a long way from the sea had to trade with those near the coast to get salt."

"But don't you see?" prompted Conchita. "It's just like your ice-cream. Just because something is poisonous doesn't mean it stays poisonous when it gets made into something else."

"How could that happen?" Greta mused. "I get what you're saying though. Come to think of it, I seem to remember that chlorine was used as poison gas in the First World War. But how can stuff lose its poison when it's made into something else?"

"It's all about chemical reactions, isn't it?" offered Phong.

"Is it? Well, I've never understood all that stuff. How can that messy lump of sodium and a gas get together to make little white grains anyway? They're just totally different things. It all seems like magic to me."

"It's atoms," explained Conchita. "I don't know how they know about atoms – I've never seen one – but I've always had a sort of picture in my head. It's like these atoms are like little people rushing around. I sort of see a sodium atom as a bully, trying to get his hands on someone else and beat them up. And chlorine's the same. When they get together, they just grab on to each other so hard they ignore anything else coming past. So if you have one sodium atom for each chlorine atom, they're all tied up and the whole lot is harmless."

"Wow!" exclaimed Phong. "That's not what I see. I think of atoms as like tiny little billiard balls …"

"Boring, compared to Conchita," cut in Greta. "Anyway, salt's natural, not like sodium and chlorine – you have to make those in a factory, don't you? I bet the sea makes its salt some other way – it doesn't do it by mixing sodium and chlorine. I reckon you have to be careful to eat only natural things if you want to be healthy."

"That's rubbish!" Phong stated forcefully. "My little brother ate some rhubarb leaves last year, and the doctor had to give him some antidote to save his life. The antidote wasn't natural, but the rhubarb was! Natural and artificial are two different things from healthy and poisonous!"

"Oh Phong, I'm sorry," wailed Greta. "I remember that time – it was awful! I didn't mean medicines – some of them are really important. But you're always seeing labels on food saying 'all natural' or 'contains no artificial ingredients' or 'chemical free'. Why else would they say that if it wasn't that it's good to have natural ingredients and bad to have chemicals?"

$\longrightarrow$

"My dad says that's all nonsense," asserted Conchita. "It's just to suck you in to buying stuff. Dad reckons everything is made of chemicals."

"Everything?" echoed Greta. "Come on – chemicals are made in factories. They're not natural but artificial. Everyone knows that!"

"Everyone?" echoed Conchita. "You certainly hear it a lot, but that doesn't mean that it's true. My dad doesn't believe it, for one. I'm not sure why he says that, but I'm going to ask him when I get home. In fact, I better go now. See ya!" Waving goodbye to her friends, she set off for home.

Discussion guides

Natural and artificial

Advertisers certainly think that customers believe natural is good, while artificial is bad. Similarly, chemicals have got a bad name, and some goods are advertised as 'chemical free'. Put these together, and it seems that artificial chemicals are among the bad things in the world.

Actually, of course, some perfectly natural products are poisonous (e.g., hemlock, toadstools) while some artificial ones are very beneficial (e.g., medicines). Some products are truthful in claiming they are natural (e.g., some 'natural therapies'), but the implication that they are beneficial can be unproven, at best. 'Natural' does not necessarily mean good, nor 'artificial' bad. Finally, everything is made of chemicals. The 92 chemical elements are the building blocks for every material thing that exists.

Does this matter? I believe it does. First, the widespread negative connotations of 'artificial' and 'chemical' do nothing to encourage students into a science or technology career. There is no doubt that *some* scientific advances are bad (see Activity 6: Are Scientists Mad?), but others are undoubtedly beneficial. Second, I believe it's important that students learn to avoid stereotyping: generalisations based on inadequate or dubious evidence. Judgements about whether a particular artificially synthesised chemical is dangerous ought to be based on the evidence, not prejudice. And the same goes for naturally occurring chemicals.

Are there any reasons for making the sorts of connections we have discussed above? We can certainly argue that any substance which has been traditionally consumed by humans may well be beneficial, or at least harmless. But examples such as tobacco and other drugs, or saturated fats, show that we must be careful: they may be harmful, or may have harmful effects in excessive amounts. Similarly, it is probably wise to require testing of new synthetic chemicals, such as medicines, before allowing their general use. The precautionary principle – that we ought to be careful about a new advance if we have any suspicions that it might cause harm – urges us to test substances before using them. (But how? See Activity 11: Animals.)

1. Is salt natural?
2. Does the answer to the previous question depend on whether it is sea salt, rock salt or salt made by combining sodium and chlorine in a factory?
3. Is salt good for you?
4. Are rhubarb leaves natural?
5. Are rhubarb leaves good for you?
6. If you are sick, is medicine good for you, even if it is made artificially?
7. Are 'natural medicines' always better for you than medicines made by pharmaceutical companies?
8. Is salt a chemical? Is water a chemical?
9. What are chemicals?
10. What things are not made of chemicals?
11. Are natural things always good? Can you think of any counter examples?
12. Should we always trust natural things?
13. Are artificial things always bad? Can you think of any counter examples?
14. Are chemicals always bad? Can you think of any counter examples?
15. Should we always distrust artificial chemicals?

Are humans a part of nature?

Notice that the natural/artificial distinction operates on an assumption that the activities of humans are not natural. Yet if humans evolved in the natural environment, like all other animals, there is a strong argument that we, and by extension our activities, are a part of nature. On the other hand, our activities are so different from those of other animals in many ways, especially through the use of tools, that there is a powerful argument that such a distinction is useful. Perhaps this human/nature distinction is helpful in some contexts, but misleading in others.

1. Are ants a part of nature?
2. Is an anthill natural or artificial?
3. Are birds a part of nature?
4. Is a bird's nest natural or artificial?
5. Is your house natural or artificial? Why?
6. If other animals change the world in some ways, and those ways are natural, why aren't the changes we humans make to the world also natural?
7. What is the difference between something that's natural and something that's artificial?
8. Are humans a part of nature, or separate from it?
9. Can you think of circumstances when it makes sense to say humans are a part of the natural world?
10. Can you think of circumstances when it makes sense to make a distinction between the natural world and an artificial, human world?

Mental models

Conchita and Phong both have models in their minds for atoms. While Conchita's is clearly not realistic, neither is Phong's because his model ignores any internal atomic structure. Indeed, Conchita's is a better model to use in explaining bonding than Phong's.

Such models can serve a purpose: they can help students to better understand some of the more theoretical parts of science. Conchita's model can be improved by positing that these 'people' can have different numbers of hands (corresponding to the chemical idea of valency), and that some of the hands are of one type (say, positive), some of a second type (say, negative), with only opposite types able to grab hold of each other. Thus, both sodium and chlorine have only one hand each, but they are of opposite types: sodium positive and chlorine negative. Once their 'hand' is held, they are unable to 'grab' (react with) anything else.

Of course, though this model helps to explain atomic bonding, it can also be misleading. Phong's model would be better in explaining how atoms bounce off each other. For students, building mental models can assist them in learning science, but they need to be wary of being misled by them. As they learn more science, they will come across more and more complex models, and it is good for them to realise that any particular model is not the same as the reality.

Models are much more important to science than just to assist students, of course. Scientists often use models. Indeed, it can be argued that, particularly in areas like chemistry, all scientific explanation is via the use of models. We can say what atoms are like, not what they are. Of course, at a high level, these models are not descriptive, like Conchita and Phong's, but mathematical.

I think students need to be aware that 'pictures' of atoms, and other scientific phenomena we offer them are often analogies, rather than descriptions of reality, with all the strengths and weaknesses that analogies have. They should know that they are often simplified, and that they will be exposed to different analogies later on. I have had senior students of science complain that they thought they understood, say, the structure of atoms, only to find that later they were offered a quite different model for the structure.

1. Are atoms little people, as Conchita says?
2. Are atoms little hard balls, as Phong says?
3. What picture of atoms do you have in your head (if any)?
4. What do atoms really look like?
5. Is it helpful to have a picture in your head to help understand how things too small to see work?
6. Is it helpful to picture something you do know about, in order to understand better something you don't know about?
7. Can having a picture in your head mislead you sometimes? Why?
8. Can one picture be better for explaining one thing, while another picture is better for explaining something else? Can you think of an example?
9. Why do we make pictures or models of things, rather than just describe them as they really are?

Activity 14 | Light my Fire

Why had those stupid teachers decided to have a school camp when winter was just starting?

They were camping out in tents this time. No nice buildings to disappear into when the weather wasn't so good, like they had last year. When they got back from their walk, it was turning cold.

Sarah, Marek and Tom were struggling to light their fire. They had plenty of wood, with quite a bit of newspaper under it, but it wouldn't light. The paper just burnt out.

"Stupid fire!" Tom spat. "Why won't it go?"

"I don't know" wailed Sarah. "I've never lit a camp fire before." None of them had. They looked enviously at a couple of groups nearby, who were huddled round their fires, which seemed to be burning much better. "Tessa!" Sarah yelled. "Come over here! We need your help."

When Tessa arrived, Marek demanded "What's wrong with our fire? Why won't it go like yours?"

"Just look at it," Tessa laughed. "You've used such big pieces of wood. It'll never go like that! You need to collect some kindling."

"What's that?" Tom asked.

"Bits of wood like twigs – we got ours from under that big tree over there. That's what you need to put on the paper, and when it starts to burn, you put on bits that are a bit bigger, then bigger still, and when it's going properly you use bigger stuff." Under Tessa's expert guidance, they soon had a nice warm fire.

"I never knew that stuff about little wood before big wood," Sarah commented, once she was warmer. "Look at that big piece I put on just now – it caught fire really quickly, but it wouldn't go at all before you came over, Tessa."

"Well, that's because the fire's a lot hotter now. Wood burns much quicker when it's hotter."

"And when it's smaller," Marek observed. "That's something new I've learnt, but why?"

"I reckon I know," chipped in Tom. "The flames can wrap around the wood more when it's small."

"What difference would that make?" Sarah asked. "I don't understand. So the wood burns faster if it's small, or if it gets hotter. Why? And is there any other way we could have got it to burn faster?" But the subject got dropped, because Mrs Sharkey had just arrived to hand out the food to cook, and they had to try to figure out how they were going to do that too – Tessa had disappeared back to her own group, and none of them had ever cooked on an open fire before.

Discussion guides

The key scientific idea underlying this story is exploration of the factors that affect the rate of a chemical reaction, that is, how fast the reaction happens. When wood burns, a series of complicated chemical reactions take place, but we can simplify them by saying that the wood reacts with oxygen in the air to produce carbon dioxide, water and ash. In the story, two factors – the size of the pieces of wood, and the temperature of the fire – are shown to affect how quickly new pieces of wood burn.

So far, our understanding of what makes a fire burn better is descriptive. It relies on observations we can make at an everyday level: the size of the wood pieces; how hot the fire seems. To move from this level to the level of scientific explanation, we must make a move that is quite common in science. We must imagine an underlying reality which is not directly observable. In this instance, we have to consider what actually happens in a chemical reaction at the atomic level.

In order to understand this, your students will need to have some grasp of atoms and molecules already. They need to know that a chemical reaction takes place when bonds between atoms are made, or broken, or both. They also need to understand that temperature is a measure of how fast atoms are moving. Then they should be able to develop an explanation for why these two factors (and others) can increase how fast a reaction, such as a burning fire, happens.

Rates of reaction and atoms

For a chemical reaction to take place, the atoms need to come very close to each other in order to bond. Smaller pieces of wood, for example, burn faster because more oxygen atoms come into close contact with these pieces. For a given amount of wood, many smaller pieces have a much larger surface area than a few big pieces, and these surfaces come into contact with the air (and the oxygen it contains) in many more places.

At higher temperatures, the atoms in both the wood and surrounding air are moving much faster, and so 'bump into' each other more often. Note: this effect is heightened because the hot, de-oxygenated air rises away from the wood so that air with more oxygen can be drawn in, and because the heat dries the moisture in the wood. Clearly, the full explanation can become quite complex!

Students might speculate on Sarah's question about other ways to get the fire burning better. One obvious way is to blow on it. Another would be to supply air with a greater concentration of oxygen – or even pure oxygen – but this might be a little too difficult and dangerous.

You may not need to ask all, or even many, of the questions below. It depends on the knowledge within your class. Your main aim will be to encourage students to consider the scientific explanations that lie behind their observations. Use your judgement about how much or how little you need to ask leading questions. Remember, it is important that students not only explore ideas that lie behind explanations of factors affecting reaction rates, but come out with scientifically sound ideas.

1. What happens when wood burns?
2. How do we explain wood burning in terms of atoms?
3. Why do the atoms of the reactants need to get close together?
4. What's the main difference between a kilogram of twigs and a 1 kilogram log?
5. Why should the fact that the twigs are thinner make a difference to how well they burn?

6. How does having smaller pieces of wood help oxygen atoms come into contact with more wood, so more burning can take place?

7. Why does wood burn better when the fire is hotter?

8. What happens to the atoms when the wood and air are hotter?

9. Why would the fact that atoms that are moving faster make them react with other atoms more quickly?

10. Can you think of any other ways you might get more oxygen atoms closer to the wood more quickly?

Observation and explanation

In the first section, the emphasis has been a specific one – about how atomic theory can explain how these two factors increase a reaction rate. Now, we can consider the very general idea that scientific explanation often works by giving an account of what we observe as humans in terms of what happens to things we can't observe directly. Appearances are explained in terms of a deeper reality.

1. What do you see when a fire starts burning?

2. Can you see the atoms?

3. Can you see the atoms making and breaking their bonds?

4. If we can't see atoms and bonds, how do we know they exist?

5. If we can't see atoms and bonds, why do scientists talk about them?

6. Are there any other scientific explanations that talk about things we can't see?

7. Why do scientists try to explain how things happen, rather than just describe accurately what they see happening?

8. Why do scientific explanations often refer to things we can't see?

Follow-up activities

1. Modelling atoms

Your students can play the parts of the different atoms, to see how various changing factors affect reaction rates. If you lack the space, numbers or time, you can use these suggestions to encourage your students to imagine what it would be like if …

The model uses a simple reaction: forming a bond between two different atoms. Split the class in two. One group are all atoms of element A, the other group of element B. They are going to react together to form a molecule of the compound AB. They do this by holding hands. If they are reluctant to hold hands, you could make some lengths of rope with a loop on each end. Those who are in group A are linked to those in group B by rope loops on their wrists. Holding hands, or linking by rope, is equivalent to a reaction which makes a molecule.

Tell the As that they are like gas atoms (say, oxygen), and the Bs that they are atoms in a solid. The As then walk around, 'bouncing' (but not violently!) off each other, the walls, etc. The Bs must stand still. When an A 'bounces' near a B, they bond and walk off together.

To see the effect of surface area, have the Bs bunch tightly together. Only those on the outside can be 'bonded' – the ones in the middle of the bunch have to wait.

To see the effect of temperature, have the As walk more quickly (but not too quick!). They will get to bump into Bs more often.

Blowing on a fire could be modelled by pushing the As toward the Bs. If your students have identified the concentration of a substance as a factor affecting the rate of a reaction (e.g., wood would burn faster in more oxygen-rich air), you can model this by putting the same number of students in a smaller area, so As bump into Bs more often.

2. Reaction experiments

There are many reactions that you can use to show how increasing surface area and increasing temperature (or other factors) will increase the rate of reaction. Most basic level chemistry texts will have some experiments. These experiments can be conducted as described.

A very simple experiment involves a candle as a heat source (a Bunsen burner is better if you have access to one), an iron nail and some iron filings. For surface area/size of the bits of iron, compare holding the end of the nail in the flame (safety: hold the other end of the nail in something that will insulate it – a peg, a wad of paper) with throwing a small pinch of iron filings through the flame. The former will show little or no effect (the nail may begin to glow eventually), the latter gives an impressive 'sparkler' display as the iron filings burn in oxygen. For temperature, you can compare what happens to the iron filings exposed to air (nothing) with what happens when the candle flame heats them.

Activity 15 | Back to the Caves

"Huh. If we listened to him, we'd all go back to the caves and live a life of misery," snorted Marek.

The speaker in assembly this week was a man from a green organisation, and he had been urging them all to 'reduce, reuse and recycle'.

"Yeah, sure," Tom sneered. "Keep on consuming Marek, and pretty soon we'll have nowhere else to live, 'cos we'll have used everything up. Like he said, we have to live in a way that's sustainable."

"I don't get it," Tessa complained. "Last week, remember, that woman from the paper mill said they will be sustainable, yet today he said we should try to use a lot less paper. Who's right? Which is really sustainable?"

"Chopping down tonnes of trees is not sustainable. You've gotta leave the forests alone, let them grow," asserted Tom.

"Yeah, but they plant new trees to replace the old. That's what sustainability is – making sure we don't run out of stuff, or that we can replace it with something else if we do," replied Marek.

"The animals can't live in the new trees, can they?" queried Tessa. "What about sustaining them?"

"But we need some paper, don't we?" Marek came back. "Sure, you can cut back a bit, but imagine going to the toilet without paper!" Everyone laughed, but they squirmed a little too.

"That woman seemed to think it was all about the economy," commented Tom. "Just as long as the companies can still make stuff, and still make money, that's sustainability."

→

"And he seemed to think it was all about keeping the environment as it is – nothing can get done that harms it in any way," responded Marek. "Don't worry if people are starving 'cos they have no job."

"Yeah, it's all very well people rabbiting on about being sustainable, but what exactly does it mean? What should we do or not do?" asked Tessa.

"Scientists can tell us," said Marek. "They can let us know what the effects on the environment are of doing this or doing that. They can calculate the risks involved."

"OK ..." wondered Tessa, "but we've still got to decide whether we ought to do it, and accept the risks, or not."

"It would help if we all lived more simply," stated Tom.

"What are you going to give up, Tom?" asked Marek, "your phone, your computer games?"

Wai Ling, who had been listening, now broke her silence. "That's alright for us," she said thoughtfully, "but what about the rest of the world? We're comfortable but we could give up a few things. There are millions of people in China, India and so on who have nothing like what we've got, and they want it. If they all got it, the environment would be a mess. But how can we tell them to keep living in poverty, so we can save the environment? If we want to save the environment, and be fair to everyone, we had better cut back a lot."

There was silence, then Marek said in a jolly voice, "OK, where's a nice comfortable cave?" They all laughed.

Discussion guides

What is sustainability?

Sustainability is clearly a good thing. Yet the idea raises a number of questions. First, what is it exactly that we are to sustain? As the term is popularly used, sustainability includes a focus on the natural world – the environment. As the characters in this story indicate, though, it can be hard to separate this out from economic and social sustainability. The word is commonly but not ubiquitously used with an emphasis on the natural world.

We might make a further distinction here between static and dynamic sustainability. The former concentrates more on keeping things as they are. To take an example from forestry: static sustainability would require all forests to be left alone. Dynamic sustainability would allow such forests to be cut down, provided new ones are planted at such a rate that we could go on cutting down forests forever. As Tessa realises, we can question whether the new forests are replacing like with like. We can ask how alike the replacement needs to be, in order to count as dynamic sustainability. Someone with an interest in the forestry industry may assume all forests are alike, while someone whose focus is animal habitats would not.

There's another twist, as Marek points out. It may not matter to dynamic sustainability if a certain resource is depleted, as long as technology gives us an alternative. If we ran out of copper to make electric wires, for example, the electronics industry can claim to be sustainable if these wires can be replaced with optic fibre.

Even if we focus only on the environment, we need to be clear about what it is that we are trying to sustain, and in what manner. Do we, for example, sustain individual creatures, species, local or global ecosystems? To focus on sustainability at one level may require not being sustainable at other levels. For example, to save a certain species may require culling a predator species. To sustain an ecosystem in a particular state may require digging up certain invasive plant species. We need to recognise that nature itself has never been a statically sustainable system. Over geological time, species and entire ecosystems have been radically changed or even wiped out. To try to 'freeze' an ecosystem is arguably not at all natural. In any case, if humans are a part of nature (see Activity 13: Unnatural Dangers), then all the changes we are making to the global ecosystem are natural. Your students might come up with distinctions like these, or they might not.

If the meaning of 'sustainability' is raised by your class, though, the discussion ought to consider just what it is that students think should be sustained, and in what manner. Is the focus purely on the environment, or on economic entities such as companies, or social entities such as communities? If we claim to want to sustain all three above, then where does the balance lie?

Are they all equally important, or should we place more emphasis on the environment or economic or social entities?

Here's the outcome you would desire. If any of your students reads a claim that such-and-such is sustainable, they will wonder what it is that is being sustained, in what sense, and what might not be being sustained as a result.

1. Tom claims that chopping down trees is not sustainable? Is he right? What is not being sustained?
2. Marek claims that planting new trees for ones that are chopped down is sustainable? Is he right? What is being sustained? Is anything not being sustained?
3. Marek also claims that it is sustainable if we run out of one thing (e.g., copper for wires) but can replace it with something else (e.g., optic fibre). Is he right? What is being sustained?
4. Who has the correct meaning of sustainability: Tom – keeping things as they are, or Marek – being able to replace things as they are used? Or is there a bit of truth in both?
5. Tessa wonders whether we can sustain one thing (trees for paper) but at the cost of not sustaining another thing (homes for animals). Is she right?
6. Marek wonders whether sustaining forests as they are might come at the cost of not sustaining people in jobs. Is he right?
7. When someone claims that a certain human activity is sustainable, what does that mean?
8. What sorts of things can be sustained?

Class activity: Types and levels of sustainability

The table opposite could be drawn on the board, and your students invited to fill it in with examples. I have given a few examples to illustrate the exercise.

Now you can allocate each student (or a small group of students) one of these entries, and ask them to write about what sustainability would mean for each entry (e.g., what would sustainability mean for Buck's wolf pack?). You could follow-up by putting the groups considering the different types at that level together, and asking them to discuss if their sustainability is compatible with sustainability of the other types (e.g., is the sustainability of Buck's wolf pack compatible with the sustainability of the Brown family, or the Blag Paper

Levels and types of sustainability

Level	Type		
	Natural	Social	Economic
Individual	A wolf called Buck	John Brown	Fred's job at Blag Paper
Small group	Buck's wolf pack	The Brown family	Blag Paper Co.
Medium group	Canadian wolves	Brownsville	The paper industry
Large group	North American mammals	The nation Brownia	Manufacturers
Biggest group	Global ecosystem	Human society	Global economy

Company?). You might also group the different levels of the same type and ask a similar question.

Class activity: How 'sustainability' is used

Ask students to find an example of a document which talks about sustainability. One way to do this, if you have internet access, is to search for the word 'sustainability'. It is best to advise students to look at deeply buried pages (e.g., ones that come between numbers 10 and 30), both because this is where they are more likely to find specific examples (instead of a general description of sustainability), and also because it will make it less likely they pick the same document. Then supply the following questions:

1. How is 'sustainability' being used in this document?
2. What type of sustainability are they talking about: natural, social or economic – or a mixture? If the latter, which type seems most important?
3. Who is using the word, and why do you think they are using it in this way?

Scientific information, risk analysis and decision making

Marek asserts that scientists can give us the information that allows us to decide whether certain human activities are sustainable or not. He lists two types: facts about the effects of the actions, and calculation of the risks involved. Tessa points out, however, that even if we know the facts and the risks, we still need to make a decision as to whether to accept the consequences and risks involved, or not.

The distinction here can be looked at as one between how the world is, or is likely to be in the future (facts) and how we think the world ought to be (values). This raises a number of questions. First, should scientists be concerned only with getting the facts straight, or should their own values influence their work? Indeed, could a scientist ever exclude their values from their work, or will values always influence what they do, even if they try to exclude them? (see also Activity 18: It's a Disaster!). Further, assuming that scientists have provided accurate facts and well calculated risks, how can we decide which way to go: accept the risks and proceed, or avoid the risks? Who should be involved in making this decision? If the activity will bring broad benefits to the wider community, with a smaller group having to bear much of the risk, should the activity go ahead or not? This last question refers to the common 'not in my backyard' (NIMBY) reaction of those who live near proposed developments. It might be understandable, but is it reasonable? We should also note that, in essence, much the same question lies at the heart of whether people in well-off countries should be forced to give up some of their advantages, so that the rest of the world can develop without such bad environmental effects (see below).

1. Marek claims that scientists can tell us the most sustainable course of action. Do you agree with him?
2. Can scientists give us facts about effects on the environment that are relevant to decisions about what to do? How?
3. Can scientists tell us what the risks are? How can they calculate this?
4. Say there is a proposal to build a factory. Should scientists argue for or against building the factory, or should they just provide us with the facts about the effects of the factory and their calculations of the risks?
5. Do you think that scientists should set aside their own views about whether a factory ought to be built or not and just give us the bare facts? Do you think they can?

6. Tessa says that 'we' have to decide what to do, which is based on the information scientists give us. Who do you think 'we' are – who ought to make such decisions?

7. Say a factory is going to produce medicines which will be very good for many people, but the main risk affects only those who live nearby. (It might make their house prices go down.) Do you think those living nearby should oppose the factory?

8. Should we accept some bad effects on us, if we know that as a result good things will happen for many others?

Follow-up activity: Risk

There are a number of aspects of risk that can form the basis of follow-up by your students.

How are risks calculated? Areas that could be investigated for risk include nuclear power, vaccinations, mobile phones, smoking, extreme weather events, volcanic eruption, tsunamis, and diseases such as cancer.

Students can search for the calculated risks for common and uncommon events such as death from various forms of transport (cars, trains, planes, bicycles, walking), lifestyle factors (smoking, drinking alcohol, obesity) or accidents (shark attacks, skydiving, rock climbing, canoeing). Comparing these can be very interesting.

The psychology of risk assessments: what are the factors that determine how bad we are at judging the relative risks of events such as death by car crash versus death from terrorism?

Environmental protection and lifestyle

Clearly, there is some tension between protecting the environment and enjoying a comfortable lifestyle. Developed countries score highly on measures of quality of life such as the UN's Human Development Index (see <http://hdr.undp.org/en/statistics/>), but they also place much greater demands on the environment on measures such as ecological footprint (Rees 1992). As a follow-up activity, your students might investigate such measures and how they work.

Developed countries such as Australia, New Zealand, the USA, Canada and many European countries have ecological footprints, which mean their citizens are making about four times the demand on nature as ecosystems can bear (Srinivasan et al. 2008). A possible implication of such information is that those living in such countries ought to reduce their load on the environment (i.e., their consumption of material goods) considerably.

There are two questions here. How willing do we say we are, and how much do we actually change our behaviour?

1. Tom says we should all live more simply. Do you agree with him?
2. How can we live more simply? What specific suggestions do you have?
3. In what ways have you chosen to live more simply?
4. If all your friends have a mobile phone, are you willing to give up your phone so as to help the environment?
5. If everyone you know is buying foods they like in the supermarket, would you be willing to give up eating foods that are produced in a way that harms the environment?
6. If all your friends' families fly or drive long distances for holidays, are you willing to only holiday at home?
7. Do you think there is a difference between what people say they would be willing to give up, and what they actually give up?

Environmental protection and the developing world

Wai Ling raises a very topical issue when she asks if the protection of the environment is compatible with fairness to those who live in the developing world. One of the major sticking points in international negotiations about climate change is the insistence by developing countries (say, China and India) that they be given much less stringent limits on their carbon dioxide emissions to continue to lift the standard of living of their citizens towards that taken for granted in the West.

However, the ecological footprint data referred to in the previous section seems to imply that raising the world's entire population to the present western standard of living would be environmentally disastrous. Should we conclude that not only do westerners need to reduce their consumption, but also that those from less developed nations cannot, and ought not, aspire to living like the average westerner does now? If so, is this fair?

Optimists think that the situation is not either/or. They believe that advances in science and technology will mean that we can find more environmentally friendly ways to improve people's lives. For example, the rising demand for electricity could be met by renewable energy sources such as solar power and wind farms. Such a view opposes the claim that it is scientific and technological innovations that have degraded the environment, and the solution is to retreat from these innovations ('go back to the caves'). No-one in the story suggests that science and technology can be part of the solution, but someone in your class may – and you can introduce the idea if no-one else does.

1. Do you think that we should try to save the environment? Why?
2. Do you think that we should help poor people in other parts of the world out of poverty? Why?
3. Do you think that it is fair that people in other countries should be able to have a similar quality of life to what you have? Why?
4. Why does Wai Ling think that getting people out of poverty and saving the environment cannot be done at the same time?
5. Do you think Wai Ling is right?
6. Which do you think should be our main aim: getting rid of poverty, or saving the environment? Why?
7. Can you think of any ways in which we could save the environment and reduce poverty at the same time?

Activity 16 | Reaction Times

"Ha! Too slow, chicken Marengo!" shouted Tom. He and Marek were playing Slaps, and he had slapped Marek's hand as he tried to pull it away for the fifth time in a row.

"I've had enough of this," Marek complained. "Let's play something else."

"You just want to stop because you can't react as fast as I can," gloated Tom. "Slow coach!"

"I'll have a go," Wai Ling offered, but Tom wasn't keen.

"You're just a girl, and everyone knows that girls aren't as fast as boys," he said.

"That's not true!" chorused Wai Ling and her friend Greta. Wai Ling continued, "I bet that I can react just as fast as you!"

"Well, let's test it out. I'll try to hit you first," Tom said.

"You're so sure that you're faster than me, why don't you let me try to hit you first?" countered Wai Ling. "After all, I won't be able to hit you, and then you can have a go at me."

"Well ... OK," conceded Tom, but he didn't look quite so sure of himself. After all, Wai Ling was the school's best squash player – boy or girl. As she proceeded to hit him time after time, Marek and Greta wandered off, chatting.

"Well, I guess that proves Tom wrong," Greta was saying. "Girls do react faster than boys!"

"Hang on – what it proves is that Wai Ling is faster than Tom," objected Marek. "And it doesn't even prove that. I was hitting Tom quite a few times before. I reckon that you've got the advantage when you're the one hitting in Slaps – you get to decide when to move and the other guy just has to react."

"Well … you might be right about that, but it's true, anyway. Girls are faster at reacting than boys."

"Are they? I wonder. How would you prove that?" Marek mused.

Discussion guides

Slaps

Slaps is a game where participants place their own hands palm to palm, and hold them out to the other player, fingertips touching. The first player then tries to slap the other's hand before the second player can pull their hands away. If the second player moves before the first player, it doesn't count. The first player continues to slap the second player until they miss, when the roles change.

Variables: Factors that have an influence

In this story, two factors that might influence reaction times are mentioned: gender and sport. However, there are many other variables that could affect the reaction time. In designing an experiment, it is important both to be able to identify variables that might be investigated, and to control any variables that might affect the outcome – but in order to investigate or control them, we need first to be aware of what they might be (see also Activities for 2: Sliding Glasses and 12: Bouncing Balls).

There is no simple way to determine in advance which variables do or don't affect an outcome. Indeed, a variable that might be very important in one situation may be quite neutral in another. For example, in the experimental design that will arise from this story, we will not be bothered if the measurements on the reaction times of different people are carried out at different locations in the room. In an experiment involving light sensors, however, location might be critical, as there might be quite different light levels at different locations. All we can do, therefore, in designing experiments is to think carefully about which factors *might* be important.

Thinking of which possible variables will need to be considered can only arise from a theory – explicit or implicit, formal or informal – of how things work. If our theory is wrong, or incomplete, we can easily overlook important factors.

Although the story raises two variables that may influence reaction time, in the discussion, students are likely to raise a number of other variables. You might like to list them on the whiteboard as they are mentioned, as they will be useful if you will later ask students to design an experiment. Being aware of possible variables will be needed both for generating hypotheses, and for thinking about how to control possible confounding variables.

1. Do you agree with Greta, that your gender affects your reaction times?
2. Do you think that the type of sport you play is related to how fast your reaction times are?
3. Are there any other factors that you could think of that affect how fast someone reacts?
4. How can we work out which variables might affect reaction time, before we do an experiment?
5. Which variables can be measured easily?
6. Which variables can be changed easily?
7. Which variables can be controlled easily?

Fair trials

The idea of a fair trial, fair test or controlled experiment comes up repeatedly in science education, and this is covered in several stories in this book. Some students will grasp the idea fairly early, though it is surprising how many students will not have thought through the idea fully. In particular, while the idea of controlling possible confounding variables can be generally understood; many students are not confident when it comes to technical details.

Students are usually initially introduced to the idea of controlling variables in situations where the experimenter has a high degree of control over a relatively simple and constrained experiment (see, for example, Activity 12: Bouncing Balls). In many situations, these matters are more complex. Reaction times are affected by a complex array of variables, many of which are not under the direct control of the experimenter.

Since the subjects of this experiment are human beings, it is either impossible, impracticable, or not ethical (maybe all three) to carry out an experiment where the same subject is tested several times, changing only a single independent variable (such as age, dominant hand, history of sports played, state of health, level of alcohol consumption). Nor it is possible to consider two different humans as being essentially identical, as we can with two tennis balls in Bouncing Balls (see Activity 12). Any investigation in which the experimenter is prevented from directly allocating values of the independent variable to randomly selected subjects is, strictly speaking, not a 'true' experiment but a quasi-experiment.

In these complex situations, there are two main ways in which the influence of confounding variables can be controlled. The first is by matching subjects so they are (near) identical on all possible confounding variables. The second is by using a large enough sample that the variations within both the groups being compared average out. In reality, most investigations students will be doing into reaction times will use a combination of these two approaches. In a single class, it is unlikely that you will be able to find two students that match closely enough to use the matched approach. Even the second approach, given the relatively small numbers of subjects available, is not ideal.

It is interesting to think about the conditions under which each of these approaches is warranted, although this might go beyond this level of schooling.

1. Was the test between Wai Ling and Tom good enough to prove that girls react faster than boys?
2. How could you modify a test between Wai Ling and Tom to make it better?
3. Could a test between Wai Ling and Tom ever answer the question as to whether girls react faster than boys? Why?
4. Would the test have been better if Greta and Marek had taken part as well? Why?
5. Any particular girl and boy are going to be different in lots of ways other than gender. Could we ever control those other variables? Why?
6. How could you design a fair test of whether girls react faster than boys?
7. What advantages would there be in trying to find a girl and a boy who are as alike as possible in every other way? How possible is this?
8. What advantages would there be in testing very large groups of girls and boys? How possible is this?

Measuring variables

Marek is right to point out that the test between Wai Ling and Tom isn't fair because they are reacting to different things: Wai Ling is reacting to her decision to slap and Tom is reacting to seeing Wai Ling move. It would be better to measure reaction times directly.

There are a number of ways you can do this, and your students may well have suggested alternatives. Some will use technology: it is relatively simple to write a program to give a signal and then measure the time it takes to press a key. Sometimes specialist equipment is available, maybe from Physical Education in your school.

However, a simple test can be done with simple equipment. The tester holds the top of a metre ruler, letting it hang vertically. The student who will be tested holds their thumb and forefinger, nearly touching the zero point either side of the bottom of the ruler. When the tester lets go of the ruler, the student grabs it. The distance the ruler has fallen before being grabbed is an indirect measure of the reaction time. You can, if you want, convert this 'drop distance' to the reaction time by using the following formula: Reaction time (in seconds) = 0.0452 x square root of drop distance (in centimetres).

Whichever way you measure the reaction time, it will become apparent that the times will vary for the same person under the same conditions for different trials. This leads to the question: how can we measure someone's 'real' reaction time, if every time we try, we get a different measurement? One of your students is likely to soon realise that we can take multiple measurements and average them, which gives a more accurate measurement.

But this raises another problem. Sometimes a student will be inattentive, and miss the initial stimulus. Their measured reaction time will be noticeably longer than the other measurements. Or they will anticipate, start reacting before the stimulus, and get an unrealistically short reaction time. Should these measurements be included in the averages? Or are they 'bad measurements' and should therefore be excluded? (It is interesting to note that in athletics, a sprinter is judged to have broken if there is too short a time (within 0.10 seconds) between the gun going off and the sprinter's first movement, even if there was no actual movement before the gun was fired.)

It is always possible that such excluded measurements may be due to effects we have not thought of, and by excluding them we miss the chance to learn.

A famous case of this sort was the failure of scientists using the NASA Nimbus-7 satellite to discover the hole in the ozone layer because a computer program had been written to discard sudden large drops in the measurements as faulty data. A British ground-based team who trusted their data came up with the discovery (see <http://www.nas.nasa.gov/About/Education/Ozone/history.html>).

While such an outcome is unlikely in your classroom, it is an issue that your students can nevertheless discuss.

1. Does the Slaps game measure reaction times?
2. How could we measure someone's reaction time more accurately?
3. What problems might there be in measuring reaction time?
4. If we measure someone's reaction time, can we be sure that the measurement is their real reaction time?
5. Is there any way we can try to ensure that we are measuring that person's real reaction time?
6. If we take several measurements and average them, will the average be more or less accurate than a single measurement?
7. If we get a different measurement every time we try to measure someone's reaction time, why might this happen?
8. If we get a different measurement every time we try to measure someone's reaction time, are some of these measurements better than others? Which ones, and why?
9. Should we try to pick out the better measurements and only average them? How can we tell which measurements are good ones, and which bad ones should we ignore?
10. If we ignore bad measurements, might we be throwing away data that could tell us something? How do we know?
11. Can we ever measure someone's reaction time precisely?

Proof

Marek wonders how you would prove that girls react faster than boys. There are several issues your students could raise from this. First, what sort of experimental evidence would count as the right type, and be enough, to establish the claim? Second, students might move on to the broader question of the nature of scientific proof.

The first of these questions depends in part on the matters discussed above. We would need to design an experiment that rules out the effects of all variables except gender. We would need to determine whether we will try for matched pairs (and what variable we would attempt to match) or, more likely, what size samples drawn from what population we will use. The latter approach requires us to try to work out how many people's reaction times we will have to measure so that we can be sure the results apply more widely than just to the sample.

Say you have a class of 12-year-olds – half girls and half boys – 24 in total. Are these two samples big enough to average out the effects of such matters as previous sporting history, state of health, body size and shape, the amount of sleep the night before and many other possible confounding variables? Even if they are big enough, can we generalise the results beyond 12-year-olds? For example, it is possible that at 12, girls are more physically mature than boys, and hence can react quicker, but that boys catch up and pass girls later. If your class is all middle class, or all Caucasian, or all well fed, would the results apply to working class, or Asian, or poorly nourished people?

Moreover, we are measuring only one specific reaction – say, grabbing a falling ruler. Would this result apply to reacting to a moving ball with a racquet, or slapping a biting mosquito, or pressing a button in response to a noise?

We can see that, whatever the outcome of the experiment we design, it is possible to question whether a better designed experiment, or one which used different equipment, or sampled more people, might give us a different result. It doesn't seem easy to prove whether girls have a faster reaction time than boys, or the opposite.

This leads to an answer to the second question above. Science sets out to establish generalisations, often in the form of laws of nature. Now, while it would be pushing it to claim that a statement such as 'Girls have a faster reaction time than boys' is a law of nature, it is a generalisation. Further, we would need to be careful about exactly what we are claiming – not 'all girls react faster than all boys', but more like 'all other things being equal, being a girl gives you a faster reaction than being a boy', or possibly 'on average, girls react faster than boys'.

Whichever way we phrase it, however, it is not possible to prove a generalisation from a finite series of observations, because some future observations could show that the generalisation does not hold after all. This is known as the problem of induction (see Activity 10: Experiments). Inductive reasoning works by observing a sufficient number of examples, and concluding that all other cases will be similar. As previously mentioned, a classic example is the observation, in Europe, that every swan is white, leading to the generalisation that all swans are white. The discovery of black swans in Australia falsified the generalisation, which until that time had seemed soundly based.

The upshot is that scientific proof is never absolute: we can never prove scientifically that a generalisation must be true. The best we can expect is that a scientific generalisation is so well supported by the evidence that it would be perverse to reject it, unless some compelling new evidence is found.

1. Marek wonders how you could prove that girls react faster than boys. How could you?
2. If we tested the reaction tines of all the boys and girls in your class, would that enable us to prove (or disprove) Greta's claim?
3. Would the conclusion we draw from such a test only apply to your age group?
4. Are there any other ways the conclusion might be limited to only people like you?
5. If we wanted to prove it one way or the other, how many people would we have to test?
6. If we make a claim that is meant to apply to all cases, past, present and future, can we ever really prove it?
7. Does this mean that we should not believe, or act on, the general claims that science makes?

Follow-up experiment

There is a wealth of possible experiments that could follow on from this story. The most obvious, of course, is to test whether there is a gender difference. However, you could follow this up, or replace it, with an experiment which tests the effects of other variables on reaction time. Your classroom discussion is likely to have identified quite a few experiments, and students can of course design their own tests.

The need for a sizable sample, though, will mean that you may need to do a series of measurements on each member of the class (and maybe beyond) so that each class member, or group, has data drawn from a large enough sample. This will require cooperation across the class, and an agreed, standardised way of collecting the data, so that it is comparable. I suggest that you devise your measurement conditions in a whole-class discussion, maybe after the groups have brainstormed methods.

Doing such an experiment will be quite demanding, and students should spend some time on careful planning. The accuracy and reliability of measurements will be limited, due both to the inherent variability of people's reaction times, and to the difficulty of making each measurement under identical circumstances. These are issues that can be discussed following the experiment.

Stages of the investigation

I suggest that you split the class into small groups of three to four students. Each group will be responsible for investigating the effect of one variable on reaction time.

Deciding which variable to investigate

Ask each group to decide on a variable that they think may affect reaction time. The variable needs to be able to be used in a classroom experiment. You can be the final judge of this, so you will be able to rule out the 'amount of alcohol consumed', for example.

As mentioned, the discussion that followed the story is likely to have suggested a good number of variables, and the groups can choose from these variables. Just in case they run out of options, here are some variables to consider suggesting to them:

- handedness (left-handers versus right-handers; preferred hand versus non-preferred hand)
- height (tall versus short)
- sport (time spent playing and training; type of sport played; sportspersons versus non-sporty persons)

- computer games (gamers versus non-gamers; type of game played; time spent playing)
- type of cue (seeing ruler drop versus eyes closed; hearing a sound as it is dropped; being touched on the shoulder as it is dropped, eyes closed)
- energy drinks (before drinking versus after drinking)
- age (does reaction time increase or decrease with age?).

It is a good idea to ask the group to make clear their reasons for thinking that their chosen variable will affect the reaction time.

They will also need to explain exactly how they will be able to collect the data they need. As can be seen from the suggestions above, it isn't enough to just identify a factor like handedness – they also have to think through precisely what it is about handedness they will measure. At this stage, the different groups may be deciding on different measurement methods for reaction times: these will need to be standardised in the next stage, since each group will be collecting data for the whole class from their own members (and maybe some people outside the class, if you all decide you need more data).

Deciding which variables to control

It is likely that your students will have previously decided that only gathering a few measurements will be insufficient to test their ideas. Hence, they will need to gather as much reliable data as they can. The obvious way to do this is for all groups to gather data from each of their members on all the variables. Some of this can be collected by asking, but all the reaction times will require a standardised method, with set ways of controlling any extraneous variables, otherwise they will not be comparable. The details of this method can be agreed with you, the final arbiter, in a class discussion. Some trial runs may be needed to identify potential problems.

Some of the decisions for students to make include:

- How will each measurement be standardised? If you are using a ruler drop, where will the ruler be held? How far apart will the fingers be? How will they ensure the ruler is 'zeroed'?
- How many measurements will be taken for each condition?

- How will they deal with 'bad' measurements – due to inattention and/or anticipation – if at all?

Gathering the data

Once the methods are decided and the variables to be collected are known, the groups can gather the needed data. The data should be recorded in such a way that they can be distributed to all groups. Writing on a master copy which is then photocopied is one possibility, or (if available) the use of computer technology. A basic spreadsheet would enable some of the calculations to be carried out more easily.

Processing the data

When the data has been collected, it will be obvious there is a large amount. How will they deal with the data? It isn't easy to see what data says when displayed like this. There will need to be some processing.

First, it will be clear that the averages need to be calculated for each single-person trial, perhaps after discarding 'bad' measurements. Then the students will need to decide what further processing is needed. When they are comparing two groups, the best way may well be to average the reaction times they now have for all the members of each group, and compare them. If the input variable is numeric (height, age, etc.), then it might be best to plot the two variables against each other on a graph and look for patterns.

These suggestions do not exhaust the possibilities. The groups might need some guidance from you in finding a good way to process their data.

Drawing conclusions

Once the students have worked out the best way to display their data, they are in a position to draw some conclusions. Yet they need to be careful here. It is a good idea to discuss their conclusions with each group separately, if you have time and opportunity, and to get them to think about how reliable their conclusion is. This will prime them for the last part, in which you can look together at the investigations and discuss the issues that can arise in trying to draw conclusions from such data. The matters the students raised in the discussion which followed the story reading may well seem more real and pressing, once students have gained some practical experience.

Discussing the results

When, in high school, students are asked to write up their experiments in a standard fashion, it often seems that the part they find most difficult is the discussion of their results. In my experience, this is also the part where they seem to have had least guidance. Most of the effort in practical work seems to go into carrying out the method and processing the results: often the conclusion is merely stated.

It is true that students are being asked to reflect on their practical work more often now. Reflection, however, is not a straightforward process, and students need guidance and practice. One of the key purposes of this book, of course, is to show you how to improve the scientific reflections of your students. As the Theory section outlined, your students' grasp of how to reflect can be improved through scaffolded discussion with their peers, before being internalised. Hence I suggest that you follow-up with a whole-class discussion of the experiment. Notes to assist you in managing the inquiry into questions the students might raise follow.

Adequacy of methods

1. How easy was it to ensure that you made all the reaction time measurements in exactly the same way? Did every group make these measurements identically? Did all groups use the same criteria for deciding which measurements to ignore?

2. What problems did you notice? (Prompts for ruler drop method: making sure the zero point and the ruler were in the same place; dropping the ruler smoothly; ensuring the subject was ready every time; having the hand that grabs the ruler in the same position every time; avoiding anticipation …)

3. How did you measure other variables? Could these methods have been made better? (Prompts: if you measured, say, time spent playing sport by asking students to estimate this time, would keeping a diary have given better results?)

4. Which variables were measured in the best way? Why?

5. Which were the most problematic? Why?

6. What suggestions would you have for overcoming those problems in this classroom? What if you had access to any equipment you wanted?

7. Are there any variables you now realise should have been controlled but weren't? How could we control them?

Accuracy of measurements

How accurate the measurements were depends a lot on the methods of measurement, as discussed above. If students use the ruler drop method, and convert the distances to times using the formula given above, their calculator will give them an answer to many decimal places. On this basis, it is not uncommon for students to claim the measurement is highly accurate.

Yet, usually they have only read the position of the fingers on the ruler to the nearest 0.5 centimetres. If your students' mathematical skills are up to it, they might calculate what the difference in time would be if the measurement were out by 0.5 centimetres. They should find that any figure after the second decimal place (hundredths of a second) means very little.

However, is even this level of accuracy justified? Students commonly find their measurements vary considerably from trial to trial, even with one subject under identical conditions. Dropping any one of the measurements from their calculations could affect their average. And so could taking another measurement. So how accurate are the measurements? You could ask your students to estimate the accuracy.

You might also ask students if taking more measurements will help.

- Would the average be more or less accurate?
- How many should we take to get an acceptable level of accuracy?
- Would a set of measurements that are very close to each other give us more confidence that we are measuring accurately?
- What should we do if we get a wide spread in the measurements? (The question of excluding some obviously bad measurements is likely to come up here as well.)

Similar issues arise for all measurements. Some measurements are more easy to make accurately than others. Depending on which data your class has decided to collect, you can ask questions like:

- Are your measurements of height more accurate than measuring hours spent watching TV? Why?

- Could you easily make your measurements of age more accurate?
- Are some things impossible to measure accurately?
- How could you get more accurate data on how much exercise people do than just asking them?

Interpretation of results

The final issue concerns the interpretation of data. A group that is investigating whether the reaction times of two groups differ (boys versus girls; sportspersons versus non-sporty persons, etc.) will almost certainly find the two averages are different. Are they warranted in concluding there is a real difference, for example, that girls are faster than boys?

The answer depends on many factors, as discussed in the Proof section above (see pp. 129–31). These factors could include whether sample sizes are big enough; whether results for 12-year-olds can be extrapolated to all ages and so on.

However, the most pressing problem here is whether the difference is significant. Scientists use sophisticated statistical tests to decide whether such differences are significant, but I am not suggesting that students either use or even learn about them at this stage. Rather, they need to be aware that such differences can arise in several ways other than there being a real difference. Here, the two most important ways to consider are: the difference arose by chance, or the difference is inside the range of measurement error.

First, we know there is some variation in reaction times of the same person under the same conditions. So, if we measured their reaction time again, we would not necessarily get the same average. They might have fluked a series of faster than usual reactions. Further, the sample of one group might by chance be unusual: we may have tested unusually fast girls and slow boys. Either of these, or a number of other factors, might mean we would not get the same result if we did another set of tests.

Second, we know that our measurements of reaction time are not completely accurate. The real value of any measurement we make is somewhere in a range between a bit higher than what we got, and a bit lower. If the averages of the two groups are close enough to lie within this range, then we cannot be sure there is a real difference between them. The more potentially inaccurate the measurements, the wider this range will be.

For data, where the comparison is between two variables that can change their values smoothly (e.g., reaction time and height), the best way to look for a relationship is usually to graph the pairs to make a scattergraph (see graphs below).

But how do we interpret the graph? If the two variables are strongly related, the points of the graph should fall on or near a clear line (16a). However, in an investigation such as this, for all the reasons mentioned above, the points your students plot are likely to scatter over the graph area. What we then need to look for is whether the points, generally, show some sort of pattern near a line. As the relationship between the two variables gets weaker, the points may be reasonably close to a line (16b), only vaguely aligned (16c), or show no real alignment (16d).

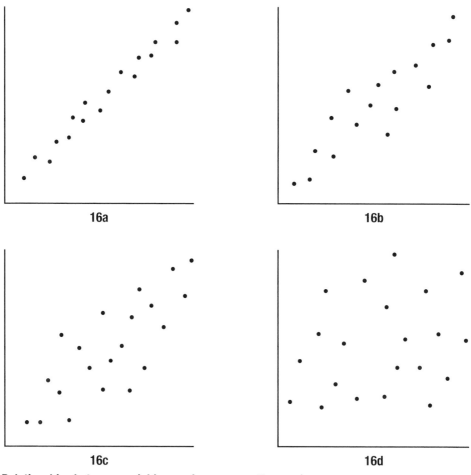

Relationships between variables as shown on scattergraphs

The same problem will arise with a scattergraph as before: if the pattern you can see in the graph is not strong, is it real, or is it merely due to sampling or measurement error? Sufficient sampling or (especially) measurement error can mask what would otherwise be a strong relationship.

The following questions are to give you a general idea of ways of assisting students to think these matters through, but they will need to be adjusted to the investigations they did.

1. What conclusion can you draw from your data?
2. If we know that our measurements are a little different each time we make them, does this mean that we cannot be sure our overall averages are accurate?
3. How big a difference does there have to be between the average reaction times for girls and boys for us to be sure that the difference is real, and not just due to flukes, or measurement error?
4. If there is a real difference between the average reaction times, but it is very small, would our investigation be able to show it?
5. Even if we have shown that girls in this class react faster than boys, can we be sure that girls in general react faster than boys?
6. Even if we have shown that girls of this age react faster than boys, can we be sure that females of all ages in general react faster than males?
7. If the points on our scattergraph do not make a line, does this mean the two variables have nothing to do with each other?
8. What reasons might there be as to why the points do not make a clear line?
9. Is it possible that there could be a relation between the variables, yet our investigation does not show it? How could that happen?

Activity 17 | Hooke's Law

Mr Carey finished giving the instructions and started to walk around the class. It was their science lesson, and he had told them to put some weights on a spring and measure the length of the spring. They had to keep measuring the length of the spring for different weights and then draw a graph showing weight against length.

Luigi was working in a group with Andy, Jenny and Greta. Andy wasn't quite sure what they had to do. "You just put the weight on, write down what it was, measure the spring and write that next to it, Andy." said Luigi. "It's easy."

At the bench where Felicity was working with Marek, Conchita and Tom, they had found a 5 kilogram weight in the drawer. Conchita suggested they hang it from the spring first, instead of the little weights Mr Carey had given them. Felicity and Marek thought they shouldn't, but Tom grabbed it before anyone could stop him. The heavy weight dropped, nearly straightening the spring and snapping it at the top before hitting the floor with a thud.

"What was that?" exclaimed Mr Carey from the other side of the room.

"Nothing," Tom said quickly. "I just knocked my bag off the bench."

"Well, it shouldn't have been on the bench," Mr Carey snapped. "That's why we have rules."

"You'll have to tell him sometime," Felicity hissed. "He'll find out that you broke his spring sooner or later."

At another bench, Sarah, Tessa, Alex and Phong were having some trouble, though they didn't realise it. Each of them was making a measurement in turn, but they did not understand between them just exactly what they were measuring. Sarah measured the spring to its bottom, while Phong was measuring only the spiral part of the spring because, as he reasoned, only that part of the spring was stretching. Alex had broken off the end of his ruler some time ago, so he'd cut it off square at the 1 centimetre mark. Now he'd forgotten about that and just put that end of the ruler at the top. Tessa was measuring with her mum's old ruler that was only marked in inches.

The class was a buzz of activity as everyone worked on the task. Mr Carey went around the room helping, though he tended to answer questions with a question of his own. Some of the students found this really annoying: they wanted to know the *answer*. When the bell rang, Tom managed to stuff the broken spring in the spring box without Mr Carey noticing and they all happily left the room for lunch break.

Alex puzzled over his science homework that night. He was pretty certain that the points on his graph ought to make a straight line, because that's usually what his science experiment graphs looked like. But his didn't. Suddenly he saw that if he drew a sort of flattish M, he could pretty well get all the points on it. As for the conclusion, he knew that Mr Carey was fond of saying: "There is a straight line relationship …", so he wrote: "There is a zigzag line relationship between weight and length."

In her room, Felicity was also having problems. She had been relieved when Tom had gotten away with having broken the spring, but now she wasn't so sure. Felicity had surreptitiously measured the stretched spring, so at least she had one point to graph, but she wondered: "How can you draw a line with only one point?" Perhaps she could draw it to where the zeros were on the graph? After thinking about that for a while, she thought it wouldn't be right, but she didn't know why.

"OK," Mr Carey said, "get your books out and we'll look at yesterday's experiment." After much shuffling, the students had their books open in front of them. "You should have found that the points on your graph made a straight line. This proves that the more weight there is on a spring, the longer it gets. That's Hooke's Law. What's more, if you double the weight, you double the length of the spring."

$\longrightarrow$

141

"But we didn't get a straight line, Mr Carey." Alex had his hand up, but he blurted out his comment before Mr Carey nodded to him.

"You have to wait until I call on you before you speak, Alex," reminded Mr Carey. "That's the law in this classroom."

"Alex's broken the law twice," sniggered someone at the back of the room.

"And we broke Hooke's Law," added Felicity, "because Tom broke the spring."

"Quiet now. I saw no hands up," barked Mr Carey. "But what's that you're saying, Felicity? Who broke the spring? *Did* you break it, Tom?"

"Yes," Tom glared at Felicity. "I just wanted to try a 5 kilogram weight."

"But Felicity's right," Luigi interjected. "If the spring broke, then they did break Hooke's Law."

"Another one without his hand up," sighed Mr Carey. "I guess we're not going to get on until I let you talk this out. OK, but let's at least try to talk one at a time. Now come on, Luigi, explain yourself."

"Well, you said that Hooke's Law is that a spring gets longer when you apply more weight. And that's what I got. I figured out this relationship …" There were a few groans around the room. Luigi was always explaining things in figures, not words, like normal people did. "First you have to take 20 millimetres off the length measurements, because that's how long the spring is to start with."

"Uhuh," said Mr Carey, trying to summarise what Luigi was saying on the board. "And then what?"

"Then you multiply the number of grams by 0.3 to get the extra millimetres you have to add on."

"Can you explain that to the others?"

"Sure," said Luigi. "The spring was 20 millimetres long to begin with and if you put x grams on it, it gets longer by 0.3 times x millimetres."

"That's explaining?" wondered Greta.

"Well, we put 500 grams on," continued Luigi, looking straight at Greta, "and it measured 170 millimetres. That's the original 20 plus 150, 'cos 150 is 0.3 x 500."

"Oh," said Greta.

"But the point is," continued Luigi, "when Felicity put ..."

"Tom put!" interjected Felicity.

"I mean, when Tom put the 5 kilogram mass on – that's 5000 grams – then the spring should have been 1520 millimetres long. But it wasn't. It broke. So that means the law is wrong."

"I measured the spring after it broke," said Felicity, "and it was 110 centimetres long."

"Well, that's because the law doesn't hold ..." started Mr Carey.

"Like the spring," muttered Tom.

"... when the weight is too heavy for the strength of the spring," continued Mr Carey, ignoring Tom. "We can't push our results past that point."

"Push our results?" echoed Felicity.

"If we only measure what happens between, say, here and here," said Mr Carey, drawing a straight line on the board, "then we can sometimes predict what will happen here," as he extended the line, "beyond where we did our measurements."

"But how do we know that will work?" asked Andy.

"We don't," interjected Luigi. "In fact with the spring it didn't."

"You're right, Luigi," continued Mr Carey. "We have to be careful whenever we push our results further because some other factor may become important, like the strength of the spring in this case."

Just then the bell went and Mr Carey told the class to pack up and leave. As he went out the door, Luigi turned to Alex and said, "Gee that was great. I wish we could talk more about our experiments. We don't usually get enough time to think about what they mean."

"Well, it didn't seem so great to me," grumbled Alex. "I never did work out why my zigzag relationship wasn't right. The experiment proved it, didn't it?"

Discussion guides

Measurement, accuracy and errors

All measurement inherently involves error, but students do not realise what this means. They often think that measurement error is merely the result of not being careful enough. Of course, this is one source of error. However, if they make their measurements carefully, avoiding this type of error, they are prone to ascribe to their measurements an accuracy that is far beyond that warranted by the method of measuring used.

In the incident in the story, the group consisting of Sarah, Tessa, Phong and Alex illustrates a number of sources of error:

- Sarah and Phong have failed to agree on exactly what should be measured. While either length – the whole spring, or only the coiled section – would give acceptable results, mixing the two lengths together would not. Similarly, if their group wishes to compare results with other groups, they need to have measured the same thing.

- The whole group has failed to agree on a standard set of units: Tessa is using inches while the others are using centimetres.

- Alex's measurements contain instrumental error. Due to a fault in the instrument of measurement (his ruler), his measurements will be systematically 1 centimetre too long.

In discussion, you can ensure that students become familiar with some of the main sources of poor measurement.

There is, however, a more pervasive sense of measurement error. The use of the word 'error' misleads many students into thinking that all measurement errors are due to such avoidable mistakes, ignoring the fact that it is impossible to avoid measurement error completely. They interpret 'error' to mean 'mistake'. Consequently, they tend to dismiss measurements which contain error as bad measurements. They need to understand that the limits to accuracy inherent in all measurements mean there will always be some unavoidable measurement error. In discussion, we should encourage students to think about whether the possible error is within acceptable limits and hence reliable enough for the purposes involved. They might also discuss the payoff between the greater costs of increasing accuracy of measurement and the adequacy of cheaper or less time-consuming measurement methods for the purposes at hand.

Activity and discussion – can we ever measure anything exactly?

Divide the class into several groups and give each group a different linear measuring instrument (e.g., 30 centimetre rule, a metre rule, a ruler marked in inches and, if you can locate any, some more unusual measuring devices). Ask them to measure the height of one member of their group as detailed below, discussing and making notes of any difficulties. Then ask groups to swap the people they are measuring so that the same person has been measured by two different groups. Comparing these measurements can be enlightening.

1. Measure the height of one group member to the nearest metre.
2. Measure their height to the nearest centimetre.
3. Measure their height to the nearest millimetre.
4. Measure their height in spans. One span is the distance between thumb tip and little finger tip in a spread out hand.
5. Measure their height exactly.
6. Convert the height measured to feet and inches, using the conversion 1 inch = 2.54 centimetres.

Now gather the whole class and discuss their findings. If the following points do not arise, you can introduce them.

1. How did you measure something longer than the measuring instrument? Did that affect how accurate your measurement could be?
2. What is the effect of the measuring instrument on the measurement?
3. Did you get the same measurements for each task as the other group? If not, why not?
4. How accurate can a measurement be? Can we keep making it more and more accurate? What are the factors that limit accuracy?
5. Were there any problems in measuring height in spans?
6. Why do we have standard units? How do we choose what the units will be?
7. How did you decide what to measure? Did you measure the person with their shoes on or off? What about their socks? Did you flatten their hair? If you took all these measurements, which measurement would be the true height?

8. What answer do you get for the conversion to feet and inches? How accurate is it?

Alternative activity

Get the class to measure the duration of some event (e.g., how long it takes a piece of paper to burn up completely). You could have a number of groups: each group uses a different method, but all members of each group independently use the same method. Here are some possible methods:

- digital stopwatches that display hundredths of a second
- mobile phones
- wristwatches
- counting the seconds
- using the wall clock.

Now gather the class to compare measurements and discuss possible sources of error. You can adapt the questions given above to help guide the discussion.

Different types of laws

The term *law* is ambiguous, and this can be confusing for students. Some laws are *prescriptive* and others *descriptive*.

A *prescriptive law* tells us what we ought to do. The laws that a government passes are prescriptive. They are able to be repealed or amended, and often have some link to moral judgements. The laws of a sport are essentially arbitrary, designed to specify how the game ought to be played. Both are instructions to people and usually carry penalties if they are not obeyed. These laws cannot be true or false, though it is perfectly possible to argue about whether they are good or just. These types of laws or rules are good if they smooth the functioning of their setting (a society, a game) and treat everyone fairly.

A *descriptive law* tells us how things happen. Scientific laws purport to describe the way the world is. Neither people nor objects can break these laws; if an event 'breaks' a scientific law, there is something wrong with the law. Scientists endeavour to determine what the true laws of the universe are. These types of laws are good if they account for all the evidence and allow us to make accurate predictions.

1. Did Alex break the law of the classroom by interrupting?
2. What happens when you break a law of the classroom?
3. What happens when you break the law of the land?
4. Did Alex break Hooke's Law when his graph did not produce a straight line?
5. Did Tom's group break Hooke's Law when the spring broke?
6. What happens when you break a scientific law?
7. What arguments might you use to support the Law of Gravity?
8. What arguments might you use to support a law against murder?
9. What arguments might you use to support a law in soccer against picking up the ball?
10. How do scientific, sports and legal laws differ?
11. Does the Law of Gravity order a stone to fall?
12. If you dropped a stone and it didn't fall, would this break the Law of Gravity?
13. If someone drove on the right-hand-side of the road in Australia, would they be breaking the law?
14. If someone drove on the right-hand-side of the road in the USA, would they be breaking the law?
15. Is the law about which side of the road you drive on decided in the same way as the law about killing other humans?

Relationships, interpolation and extrapolation

Two variables are related if one changes in a predictable way as the other changes. It isn't often possible to continuously change one variable and watch the other change smoothly. Rather, we take a number of fixed values of the independent variable and then measure the corresponding values of the dependent variable. The most common way to check whether there is a relationship is to graph the two variables against each other, and look to see if there is a simple shape to the graph.

The simplest shape is a straight line, and it is often the relationship that we find in the sorts of experiments carried out in school science. However, it is not uncommon that when students plot measurements they have made on a graph, the points do not line up exactly on a straight line. What then is the justification for drawing a straight line, rather than joining all points – something students are prone to do? It is because we can assume that there has been some measurement error. If the 'real' values had been measured, then all points would have fallen precisely on the straight line. If the errors get too large, of course, they can obscure the actual relationship between the variables.

1. Was Alex justified in drawing the zigzag line joining his data points on his graph?
2. Is Alex right to think that the points on a graph ought to form a straight line?
3. Why don't we just join each point on the graph to the next?
4. If the data points do not quite make a straight line, then what justification do we have for drawing a straight line that doesn't pass through all the points?
5. Could Felicity draw her graph using the one point she measured and the zero points?
6. If we only need two points to draw a straight line, then why do we need to collect data for more points?
7. When do you draw a straight line and when do you draw a curve?
8. When a point doesn't seem to lie on a line, how can we distinguish between these two possibilities? (1) That point was measured badly (e.g., getting the length of the spring wrong); (2) That point shows that something else is happening (e.g., the spring doesn't obey Hooke's Law for some reason we haven't considered).

In drawing a simple shape like a straight line to join the points obtained, an assumption is made about the values in between that were not measured: they would vary smoothly in between the values actually measured. The straight line can be used to predict what the intermediate measurements ought to be, so we use the line to work out the value at C, in between A and B (see graph opposite). Technically, this is called interpolation of the values.

If we extend the line beyond the limits of the values we have measured, to predict the values at D (i.e., we extrapolate), we are making a similar assumption that the values will continue to vary smoothly following the same pattern outside the range we chose to measure.

These assumptions are usually unstated, and are often justified. However, as the story shows, we are often safer interpolating than extrapolating. The assumptions break down when some other factor, which we have not considered, comes into play. In the story, the 5 kilogram weight exceeds the strength of the spring, so the spring breaks. After breaking point, there is no longer any relationship between weight and length.

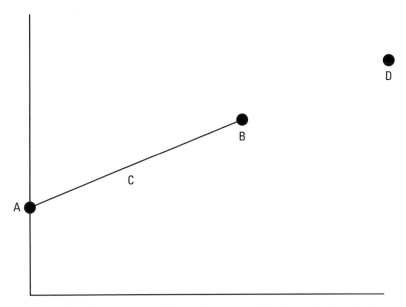

Graph plotting the independent variable against the dependent variable

1. If Luigi has measured the length of the spring as 140 mm when 400 g is added, and as 200 mm when 600 g is added, then how can he tell how long the spring would have been if he had added 500 g?

2. Do you think that working out in-between lengths like this is reliable? Why?

3. If we really want to study how the spring gets longer as we add more weight, why don't we continuously add weight to the spring, rather than just picking out a few weights?

4. Say Luigi has measured the length of the spring as 140 mm when 400 g is added and as 200 mm when 600 g is added. Can he then predict accurately how long the spring will be if he adds 1000 g? Why, or why not?

5. Why does Felicity say Tom broke Hooke's Law?

6. Did Tom break Hooke's Law?

7. Mr Carey says that if we double the weight on a spring, we double its length. Is he right?

8. Which is more reliable: predicting in between measurements, or predicting measurements beyond our experimental data? Why?

Explaining and understanding

Central to the scientific endeavour (and other endeavours) are the concepts of explaining and understanding. If your students are to gain a scientific outlook on the world, then it is essential that they not only know scientific facts but also see the importance of seeking and understanding explanations that are scientific. Yet many students seem to feel that science is merely a matter of being able to repeat facts (this is not entirely their fault, as science examinations can fall into the same trap).

Explaining may well be a different sort of thing in different disciplines. For example, a historical explanation may involve reference to people's goals and desires. We would not talk about the goals of the spring or weights in this experiment. So, what is distinctive about scientific explanation? This is not as straightforward a matter as we might think. There are several possible answers to this question. How deeply you can go into the matter with your students is a judgement for you to make.

Sometimes explanation seems merely to involve giving a scientific term to an everyday occurrence. Why does a stone fall when unsupported? The answer is gravity. If 'gravity' is nothing more than a fancy name for 'unsupported objects fall', we do not adequately explain why the stone fell at all. Renaming is not explaining. Rather, it is describing, using specialist terms.

Perhaps explaining is providing a mathematical relationship between two variables, such as Luigi does in the story. While Luigi has described this relationship in words, scientists commonly use a mathematical shorthand, such as the equation $L = 20 + 0.3W$ (where L represents the length of the spring in millimetres, and W the weight in grams). Does this equation explain the way the weight is added and how this relates to the length of the spring? We could see such a mathematical relationship as nothing more than a fancier renaming or redescription. The equation merely describes, in mathematical terms (albeit in a more exact way), what happens to the spring as the weight increases.

This may be a little too glib. Luigi did not give Hooke's Law as such but a particular application of it. If we generalise this equation, replacing the 20 with a symbol for original length (say, L_0), and the 0.3 with a symbol for a constant (say, k), then using Hooke's Law to explain the extension of this spring is showing how this particular situation (the spring with weights hanging off) fits into a general law (Hooke's Law: $L = L_0 + kW$, which covers the way all sorts of objects get longer under stress). This is certainly one type of explanation: showing how a particular event falls under a general rule.

Further, by writing an equation, we are able to make predictions about the future and thus far untested behaviour of the spring. Thus the claim can be made that we understand how the spring works: we have an explanation for what it will do in general.

However, although such equations describe a certain case as a type of general phenomenon, there is a sense in which it does not tell us *why* the spring stretches – merely the *way* it stretches. An explanation then may require that we give a mechanism for the event.

In science, this sort of mechanical explanation commonly means reinterpreting what we can observe in terms of a model. Scientific models are often based on unobservable events (see also Activities for 4: Seeing Things and 14: Light my Fire). So, the elasticity of the spring can be explained by a model at the atomic level, which refers to what happens to the bonds between atoms when stress is applied. Such a model, however, only works well if it is cast in terms of familiar events. In the case of stretching a spring, the model appeals to a familiar event – the event we are trying to explain! That is, we think of the bonds between atoms as being like little springs. When we stress them, they lengthen, and return to their original shape when the stress is released. So perhaps, at least in this case, this sort of explanation is circular.

Clearly, the concept of explanation is not straightforward. Perhaps what we will allow to count as an explanation depends on the context in which we ask for explanation.

1. If I ask you why a stone falls when I let it go, and you say 'gravity', have you explained why the stone falls?
2. If I give a scientific name to something that happens, have I explained it?
3. When Luigi gives a way of calculating the results from the experiment, is he explaining the stretching of the spring, or is he describing it?
4. If we show that the way this spring stretches obeys Hooke's Law, are we explaining how the spring stretches?

5. If we can use an equation to predict what the spring will do under future loads, have we explained the stretching of the spring?

6. Does knowing an equation that covers the way in which a spring stretches mean that you understand why it stretches the way it does?

7. Is there a difference between understanding how and understanding why?

8. What sort of story would count as an explanation of why the spring stretches the way it does?

9. Would it help to refer to atoms and how they bond together?

10. If atoms are too small to be seen, and the bonds between them are invisible, how can we understand an explanation that refers to them?

11. If we have an explanation of the spring that talks about bonds between atoms stretching and returning to their original length, do we have an explanation of why bonds act like that?

The purpose of an explanation, of course, is to provide understanding. If there are different types of explanation, though, there may well be different levels of understanding too. An explanation that satisfies now may not be sufficient later. This raises the question as to whether we can ever reach a full understanding of a scientific phenomenon, or whether there will always be more questions.

1. Did you understand Luigi's explanation of Hooke's Law?

2. Do you understand how to raise your hand?

3. Do you understand all the events that take place in your ears, brain and body between being asked to raise your hand, and your hand going up?

4. If you understand an explanation, how can you prove to yourself that you understand it?

5. If you understand an explanation, how can you prove to other people that you understand it?

6. Could you understand an explanation and yet not be able to explain it to someone else?

7. Could you think you understand an explanation now, but later find out that you didn't really understand it?

8. If your teacher explains something to you and you don't understand it, whose fault is it? Is it the teacher's? Is it yours? Why?

9. What methods can you use to help you understand an explanation better?

10. Is it possible to understand things in different ways, or at different levels?

11. Can you ever fully understand anything?

Follow-up experiment

You can follow-up this story by asking your students to do the same experiment. The necessary equipment is probably at hand in a secondary school, but may be harder to locate in a primary school. You will need:

- an appropriate number of small, lightweight springs
- a set of 50 gram weights and weight hangers
- somewhere to hang the springs from
- rulers
- graph paper, pencils.

With your class, you can discuss how they are going to go about carrying out the experiment, which is pretty straightforward. There will be a need to decide what values they are going to choose for the weights to hang on the springs. Ask the students to draw up a graph, with the weight added on the horizontal axis, and the length of the spring on the vertical axis.

Once the graph has been drawn, you can ask students to predict the length of the spring for weights they didn't use – both within their testing range (interpolation) and beyond (extrapolation).

You can, if you wish, allow the class to try to find the point at which Hooke's Law starts to fail. However, be warned that the springs will not be able to return to their original shapes after such testing, and so will not be useful in the future.

Extensions

Like most science lessons in middle schooling, this story makes some simplifications. In particular, the story does not deal with the following matters, which you might like to introduce if your class is at the older end, which include:

- the distinction between the weight of an object (measured here in grams or kilograms) and the gravitational force acting on it (measured in newtons)

- more sophisticated graphing, including the derivation of a simple linear algebraic equation from the graph drawn, linking weight and length of the spring
- explicit use of the terms 'interpolate' and 'extrapolate' to talk about pushing results beyond the actual measurements made.

Of course, even younger students may be able to cope with some of these ideas, even if they have not covered these ideas formally elsewhere, with some help from you and some research. Whether to introduce some or all of them to your class is your decision.

Activity 18 | It's a Disaster!

"Those people had no chance!" Tom exclaimed. "That earthquake hit without warning." He waved the paper's headline about a damaging tremor near a sizable town on the other side of the country.

"Why didn't those scientists – wotchacallem, who study earthquakes – tell them it was going to happen?" asked Greta.

"Seismologists," offered Tom, who always seemed to know these things. "They didn't because no-one can predict earthquakes. They just happen at random."

"Come on," interjected Alex, "we learned about how earthquakes come from all that pressure in the rocks building up, then they just crack. So if they measure the pressure, surely they can predict the earthquake."

"I guess they try," replied Tom, "but it's too complicated. They might be able to tell something's gonna happen sometime in the next few years, but they can't tell exactly when."

"I heard that seismologists in China look at animals – when dogs get frightened, they know the earthquake is about to happen," said Wai Ling, "but it doesn't always work."

"It's like that flood we had," Conchita asserted. "The weatherman said it would rain, but they never told us we'd get washed out."

"Well, the weather's complex too," Alex pointed out. "It's hard to predict precisely."

"In our science lessons, all our experiments are meant to be precise, aren't they?" mused Wai Ling. "How come those experts with all their training can't get it right?"

→

"How do they try to predict earthquakes and weather and climate and stuff like that anyway?"

"Models," explained Alex. "They use a computer to make like a pretend earth – a bit like SimCity® or SimEarth® or something – and then they run it to see what happens in the future."

"How do they know their model acts like a the real world?" Conchita asked.

"Gee, I don't know … I guess they don't really," conceded Alex.

"I reckon they're biased," Greta stated. "Look at all those scientists going on about global warming – they're just trying to scare us, so they can make more money from their work. They predict what suits them."

"Huh," snorted Tom, "it's the other way around. All those scientists who reckon it isn't happening make their money from the oil industry. They're the ones who are biased."

"Yeah – it's just like research funded by the dairy industry tells you how much better butter is for your health than margarine, and the margarine manufacturers get research done that proves the opposite," added Alex.

"Every scientist has to raise money from somewhere," Emma reasoned. "Does that mean they are all biased?"

"They shouldn't be," Wai Ling stated. "Science is meant to be unbiased. Anybody researching the same stuff should get the same answer, just like Mr Carey says we should all get the same answer in class."

"Well, they don't," complained Conchita. "I just don't know who to believe on global warming. How can you work out who's telling the truth?"

Discussion guides

Complexity, models and prediction

Science does not have a single scientific method (see Activity 8: Dinosaurs) – rather, it uses many methodologies. School science can leave the impression that controlled variable experiments are the only 'real' way to do science.

Many of the phenomena studied by scientists are too large and complex to utilise experimental work undertaken in laboratories, though such experiments can help tease out underlying principles. In cases such as geological phenomena, weather systems and climate (considered worldwide over centuries or millennia), a realistic, full-scale, real-time experiment cannot be carried out. The variables involved are not susceptible to manipulation: meteorologists, for example, cannot re-run a hurricane with a different input of solar heating, just to see what would change.

In such cases, scientists turn to different methods. One method is to use natural experiments. Scientists can measure and study similar events – say, many hurricanes – each of which will arise in slightly different circumstances. By teasing out the different initial conditions, and applying theories developed in laboratory studies, they can speculate about how changes in a particular variable result in different outcomes – say, a stronger or longer lasting hurricane.

As their understanding of a phenomenon grows, scientists often construct a mathematical model. Such modelling has been greatly enhanced by the availability of powerful computers. Let's look at a weather model as an example. Meteorologists will try to write a set of equations that describe how certain initial conditions (temperature, air pressure, wind speeds and so on) will affect each other as time passes. These new values give scientists a forecast of what the weather may be. Models are usually tested by feeding in values from the past, and seeing if the model predicts the weather that actually happened. If it does, then we have grounds for believing that its predictions in the future may be accurate.

Of course, this model is a simplification of real world weather in a number of ways. First, the mechanism involved in, say, how temperature affects wind speed, may not be fully understood, so scientists use an approximation of the process. Second, the vast amount of data needed to describe initial systems fully means that scientists use average values over particular areas. An example: the wind speed and direction in a valley will change depending on where in the valley you are located, but the model will use an average speed and direction over the whole valley. Third, when the model fails to predict past events well, scientists may 'tweak' the model, by introducing changes that have little theoretical basis, but improve the model's predictive ability on known events.

Hence, scientists may well use a number of models, each of which has performed well in certain tests, and then use the outcomes produced by the majority of models as a basis for their predictions. It is easy to see that such predictions will have inbuilt uncertainties, so scientists will often give a range within which the outcome will probably lie, given certain conditions, or give a percentage likelihood of the outcome. An example for the former approach is the Intergovernmental Panel on Climate Change (IPCC) report in 2007 (available at <http://www.ipcc.ch/>), which predicts a global mean temperature rise of 1.4°C to 6.4°C by 2100, given rapid economic growth. For the latter approach, weather forecasters may give a probability of 70 per cent that it will rain on a certain day.

Understanding the limitations on the accuracy of computer modelling ought to be an important aim of the discussion. There are practical limits on the accuracy and detail of data that can be collected and input into models; uncertainties in the accuracy of the complex scientific theories used; questions as to whether all relevant factors have been recognised and taken into account; doubts about how different aspects of the situations interact; and a lack of knowledge of new events or changes which might intervene in these processes. While improved models may reduce uncertainties and lead to more accurate predictions, absolute accuracy is not obtainable.

Of course, scientists realise this, and always give some indication of margins for error in the predictions their models make. However, others such as reporters, politicians and the general public, do not always pay attention to these uncertainties, and can then blame scientists when the prediction turns out to be somewhat inaccurate, even if the inaccuracy falls within the error margin. Further, people often mistake the level of detail and applicability of a model, for example, when they assume that a prediction of a long-term increase in the average temperature of the atmosphere means each day is going to be warmer than it was last year.

It is easy to see why school students do not create models in their science lessons in the middle school years. The phenomena that call for modelling are too complex, and the science behind the various processes that interact are too advanced for students at this level. However, this does not mean they are unfamiliar with computer modelling: many computer games have at their core a mathematical model of some aspect of the world. ProFlightSimulator®, for example, models how an aircraft responds to both the external conditions and the actions of the pilot, and virtually every game models how the appearances of objects change as the player moves to another position.

1. Is Conchita right when she says that the weather forecasters don't give us accurate forecasts? Why do you think that is?
2. Do you agree with Alex that the weather is complex? What sorts of factors make it complex?
3. Is Tom right when he says forecasting things like earthquakes is hard because these events are too complicated?
4. Do you agree with Wai Ling that science is precise?
5. Why can't scientists studying earthquakes, weather and climate be precise and accurate?
6. Why can't meteorologists (weather scientists) do experiments to find out exactly how the weather works?
7. If you can't make an experiment about the weather where you test one variable at a time, controlling all the others, then how can you work out the science of weather?
8. What do you think Alex means when he says scientists use computer models to study complex events like earthquakes, weather and climate?
9. How would you make a model of the weather?
10. Have you ever seen a computer used to model some aspect of the world? In what ways do computer games model the world?
11. Are the models of the world in computer games just like the real things they model? How accurate are they?
12. Can you suggest reasons why a computer model of (say) the weather is not as accurate as the real weather?
13. Can you think of any ways in which computer models can be made more accurate?
14. If we know that computer models have limits on their accuracy, then how should we use their predictions to make decisions – for example, about climate change?

Bias in science

Both Greta and Tom accuse certain groups of scientists of bias, based on historical examples. Greta: after the leaking of emails from the Climate Research Unit at the University of East Anglia in November 2009, climate scientists were accused of a conspiracy to exaggerate claims of climate change (*The Guardian*, 20 November 2009). Tom: a headline in *The Guardian* newspaper of 27 January 2005 in the UK reports on allegations that 'Oil firms fund climate change "denial"'.

Climate change is not the only area where scientists are accused of being biased, often in response to funding sources for their work. As Alex notes, studies into the health benefits of various foods often seem to be funded by the industry that produces the food, and a meta-analysis of such studies by Lenard Lesser and colleagues (2007) concluded that industry funding may bias conclusions in favour of sponsors' products. Similar findings have been made in drug testing funded by pharmaceutical companies.

There are two major questions here:

1. What are the sources of such alleged bias?
2. Is it possible for scientists to avoid bias altogether?

To take the first question: clearly one possibility is that some scientists deliberately skew their research to give the result their sponsor would want. No doubt this sometimes happens. Of course, scientific results are meant to be replicable, and other scientists will try to replicate contentious results. In such cases, the misuse of scientific methods is likely to come to light. However, not all experiments are replicated – someone else would need to have both the inclination and the funding to want to replicate it – and so these results may stand unquestioned (Zimmer 2011). This is especially likely when the rest of the scientific community thinks the results are uncontentious, or of little interest. In one famous case of failed replication, it was up to two 14-year-old New Zealand science students to try to replicate measurements of vitamin C content in a commercial fruit drink, and to discover that claims on the packaging were wrong, see <http://www.guardian.co.uk/world/2007/mar/27/schoolsworldwide.foodanddrink>. (While the company was fined for false advertising, I do not wish to imply this was a case of deliberate fraud by scientists – rather, it is an example of claims of too little interest for other scientists to test.)

However, not all cases of bias are due to deliberate falsification of results. Sometimes it occurs through the choice, for example, of whether or not to publish the results of experiments. This was one of the charges levelled against the Climate Research Unit: that they failed to publish, and tried to hide, data that discounted their claims that humans caused global warming. (Investigations found little evidence that such malpractice occurred.)

Currently, this is a matter of concern with drug testing by pharmaceutical companies. Recent work (Rising et al. 2008) shows that companies tend to publish experiments only when they show the results the company wants. Thus, the publicly available record of research on the drug is incomplete and biased. Regulators in several countries are moving to make drug companies publish the results of all their testing: positive, negative and inconclusive.

Finally, there are many factors which can lead to unintentional bias. Broadly speaking, we can separate them into two groups: those factors to do with a subconscious leaning towards evidence that supports the scientist's expectation (experimenter bias) and those that arise from experimental designs that inadvertently introduce bias (design bias). Some of these factors are discussed in Reaction Times (see Activity 16). Since good experimental design is aimed at eliminating all forms of bias, including experimenter bias, these are not completely separate categories.

With regard to experiments, much work has gone into developing robust designs which, as much as possible, eliminate the possibility of such unintentional biases. In other activities we have looked at the idea of a *fair test*, designed to eliminate the possibility that the effects we are seeing are due to some variable other than the one we think we are studying. As we saw in Activity 10: Experiments, we can never be entirely sure that we have considered all the variables we ought to have considered. This alerts us to the realisation that some bias is always possible, no matter how careful we are.

In experiments where human subjects are involved (such as testing the efficacy of a new drug), double-blind experiments are meant to remove all opportunity for human bias. Drugs are tested by comparing their effects to those of an ineffective alternative such as a sugar pill. Since we know that a patient's expectations can make them get better (the placebo effect), we need to ensure that none of the subjects of the experiment know whether they are taking the drug or the sugar pill. They are therefore 'blind' to what they are taking. Similarly, we know that an experimenter can subconsciously treat those taking the drug (the experimental group) differently from those taking the sugar pill (the control group), producing different outcomes. Hence, we need to ensure that those who are interacting with patients are also 'blind' as to who takes what. In good designs, the people analysing the result are also kept unaware of which group subjects are in until the analysis is complete.

The use of mathematical models introduces further complications. As they are not experiments, but rather linked mathematical equations devised by scientists, the above techniques won't work. In deciding such matters as to which factors their model should include, and how much relative weight to give them, there is a good deal of room for subjective decisions, and hence either deliberate or inadvertent bias. One way to check for bias is to test models against measurements taken in the past, to see if the model can match them – but this does not ensure it will match future measurements. A second way is for different scientists around the world to compare their models, and to place more trust in those that agree with each other. Of course, opponents of the human-induced climate change theory have alleged that models agree due to a conspiracy.

Scientists, of course, are human. They are always interested in which way their experiments and models turn out, and they prefer the results to fit with their hypotheses, which capture their expectations of how the world works. Nevertheless, in order to be good scientists, they need to present objective results, and the best way to obtain results is to carefully think through how to devise and test models, and carry out experiments, so as to try to neutralise bias.

In the discussion plan that follows, some of the questions invite speculation about these matters, and students may well not be able to come up with anti-bias techniques that have been developed over centuries of scientific research. This provides a great opportunity for a research project: see follow-up activities at the end of this activity.

1. Greta, Tom and Alex give examples where they think scientists are biased. Do you think scientists are biased?

2. Why might research that has been funded by a certain industry produce results that favour the industry's products?
3. If two scientists studying the same phenomenon disagree, does that mean that one (or both) of them is biased?
4. How could we check if a scientist's work is biased?
5. Scientists usually have a hypothesis – they expect that the world works in a certain way. Does this mean they are always biased?
6. Is it possible to be biased without meaning to be?
7. How can scientists guard against being biased?

Conflicting scientific views

Conchita wonders who is telling the truth about global warming. She is not alone. The media are full of conflicting stories on the issue, often quoting 'experts' who have quite different views as to whether global warming is occurring, whether the warming is due to human activity, the extent of the warming, the effects of a certain level of warming, and what we ought to do in order to ameliorate the effects and so on.

Global warming is only one of many contentious scientific issues, where uncovering the truth is important and relevant to decisions about our everyday lives. Others include what the health benefits or dangers of certain foods or behaviours are, whether certain drugs should be allowed to be sold, whether planes should be allowed to fly while volcanoes are erupting nearby, what the dangers are in building houses in flood or earthquake prone areas – and many others.

If the experts disagree, then how do we know who to pay attention to? There are no easy answers here, yet decisions have to be made. So let's look at some of the possible factors.

First, we can consider whether any of the experts are likely to be biased, as we did above. Who funded their research? There is a problem here, though. Just because the findings of research funded by an interested body are favourable to that cause, it does not follow that the results are wrong. If scientists have a public commitment to certain actions (e.g., climate scientists who urge us to switch from fossil fuels to renewable energy), should we therefore suspect they are coming up with findings that fit their political views? However, the political views might have been produced by scientific findings rather than vice versa. Other indicators of possible bias are also inconclusive: we might be suspicious of bias, but it is hard to prove.

Maybe we should look to see what the majority of scientists claim. If a large majority who have studied the phenomenon agree, then surely that is the sensible view. This is the way science is supposed to work in complex issues: many scientists work on the problem, some make small breakthroughs and others make mistakes. Gradually, mistakes are weeded out because others cannot replicate them, and breakthroughs are connected into a solid theory, on which almost all converge.

Again, there is a problem. In the past, scientists have converged on a theory (e.g., that space and time are absolutes, continents are fixed in position, or species are individually created), only to have that theory overturned by a new insight. Yet, for a while, the majority of scientists stick to the theory they know, and which has been successful for them. Peer pressure is powerful, and only a brave few (who are sometimes wrong, of course!) stand up for a different theory. Indeed, in modern science, where results need to be published in a reputable scientific journal following review by other scientists, there is a worry that new or minority theories do not get a fair hearing because the majority do not agree with them. (One of the allegations against the Climate Research Unit was that they were urging colleagues not to allow opposing work on climate change to be published.) So, while the agreement of most scientists can be a good indicator of the truth, it is not infallible.

So perhaps we have to check the research and arguments of scientists ourselves, to see if both hold together. The problem here is that modern science at the cutting edge is complex, and we would need to learn a great deal before our judgements can be solid. Yet, if we do become experts, it is likely we will have become committed to certain theories. Now others will question our judgements. In any case, the dedication needed to learn one area of science will rule us out from becoming an expert in other areas.

Clearly, there is no simple solution. The best we can do, perhaps, is to try to develop a good general understanding of how science works, acquire some knowledge in areas of interest to us, and go along with the best scientific consensus we can find, for the time being.

Meanwhile, we should keep in mind the possibility that we could be wrong, so that we consider opposing arguments, looking to see whether they are compelling enough to warrant changing our mind. This is one central element of a scientific attitude. Developing it in your students is one of the aims of this book.

1. Conchita wonders who is telling the truth about global warming. Do you sometimes have trouble deciding who to believe?
2. Can you think of any other situations where different people have different opinions on a scientific issue?
3. Why might two scientists have different opinions on the same scientific matter?
4. If two scientists disagree, does this mean one of them is biased?
5. How can you tell if a scientist is biased?
6. If most scientists believe in one answer to a scientific problem, and a few believe in another, should we accept what the majority believes? Why?
7. Can you think of any examples of times when most scientists believed in one answer, but they turned out to be wrong?
8. If we want to know which scientific opinion to believe, should we do the investigation ourselves?
9. Can you think of any problems we might have in trying to work out for ourselves which scientific answer is right?
10. When scientists disagree, how can we decide who we ought to believe?

Follow-up activities

Each of the three areas for discussion mentioned above provides ample opportunities for student research before, during or after class discussion. Much of what they find – particularly on the web – may be too detailed for them to fully understand, but it will certainly feed more information into their discussion.

While students are not going to be able to understand and analyse sophisticated mathematical models, they can certainly do some research to find out more about the process, and also to discover some of the factors that are included in particular types of models. For example, for the weather, they could find out about how such models calculate the possible future weather by dividing the earth's surface into 'cells' and determining how each cell changes over time, and how it affects neighbouring cells. Similarly, they could find out which parameters – temperature, wind direction, humidity – are included in the model.

Questions of bias open further research opportunities. You could set your students to do a web investigation of matters such as cases of scientific fraud, sources of research bias, double-blind testing, mathematical models that do not agree and so on, and report back what they have found.

Finally, students could look for cases of scientific controversy that are new to them. Newspapers provide a steady stream of examples, although students may find, in their research, that the scientific consensus is much stronger than the media portray in some areas, such as humans causing global warming. Finding articles that sum up balanced evidence (or a pair of articles that take opposing sides) can introduce more information into student discussions.

Conclusion

Where to for science education?

'Science education in Australia, as in other post-industrial countries, is in a state of crisis.' These are Russell Tytler's opening words in an influential review entitled *Re-imagining science education* (2007, p. 1), based on a conference organised by the Australian Council for Educational Research in 2006. Tytler concludes that, as the importance of science to society has grown, its educational effectiveness in schools has waned. Much has been written about the reasons – some were discussed in my Introduction.

Solving this crisis through re-imagining science education is a major undertaking which needs to occur at many levels. Clearly, governments and educational authorities have a role to play, in modifying curricula and providing funding for large-scale projects. While this role is important, it is not enough. Moreover, excellent programs are at the mercy of political decisions and can be cut, no matter how successful they are – witness the recent axing of Primary Connections and Science by Doing in Australia. For real, effective change, clearly we cannot rely on governments: lasting reform must take place at the chalkface.

This book encourages you to play your part in the reinvigoration of science education in your classroom. You as teachers are at the heart of science education: what you do with your students is of vital importance to their attitude to, and grasp of, science. This means that you may need to take on new teaching methods, to supplement the successful ones you already have. As Tytler (2007, p. 64) puts it, 'Teaching strategies in science need to be more varied, with greater agency accorded to students to pursue ideas and have input into discussion.' This book provides guidance and materials to aid you to incorporate the scientific community of inquiry into your teaching repertoire.

No one pedagogical approach is capable of providing a great science education, and this includes the one advocated here. You will need to exercise professional judgement about the appropriate time and context in which to use this approach, and how best to mix it with lectures, readings from textbooks, practical experiments, research projects and other activities.

Nevertheless, I believe your science activities can be greatly enriched by conducting rich, yet rigorous discussions with your students. While it may seem that, in relinquishing your role of fount of all scientific knowledge, you are withdrawing from the teacher's central role, nothing could be further from the truth. Your guiding role in the discussion, monitoring carefully what is said, is to encourage and cue fruitful moves on the part of students, to model explicit and reflective thinking, and so on. This is central to the success of inquiry centred teaching and learning.

What are we aiming for in teaching science? Certainly, we want our students to have a wide knowledge of scientific facts, theories and explanations and to be skilful in carrying out scientific investigations. Yet we should aim for more.

I have argued that discussions in your science lessons offer you ways of assisting students to:

- deepen their understanding of scientific concepts
- strengthen their ability to think scientifically
- grasp the many ways in which scientists and scientific methods work
- see how science draws on creativity, emotions, intuitions and imagination
- situate scientific knowledge in the wider context of their everyday lives
- apply their general knowledge of science to unfamiliar social situations that involve science
- grasp how working collaboratively can build science understanding.

A successful solution to the crisis in science education depends heavily on teachers: that is, on us. We must learn how to further engage students in science. We need to add to our range of teaching strategies in ways that allow students to voice their own ideas, enthusiasms, fears and concerns. We need to diversify our teaching strategies in ways that involve all students in a critical survey of what science is, how it works, and what it can and can't achieve.

In doing so, we do not want to abandon some of the major insights that science has provided to society. Nor do we want to neglect equipping students with the practical skills to carry out scientific investigations. The main thrust of this book is not to strengthen only these areas. It is about adding further value to science education, in a way that appeals to more students, and encourages them to see what a great and central role science plays, yet arms them with the tools to see science through discerning eyes, so they can weigh up the balance of what science offers and the pitfalls.

I have offered you a range of activities to achieve these aims. Each involves a specific content area of science and not all content areas are covered. A book that provides stories and discussion guides for all the content in science syllabuses in the middle years of schooling would be lengthy indeed.

If you like the activities offered here and wish you had more, I urge you to think about what you can do to engage your class in a community of inquiry in other areas. Indeed, if you are successful in creating a scientific community of inquiry using these stories, you may well find what I have found in my own classrooms: students will move from what they are doing into a discussion as the need arises. These communities of inquiry may start with a specific question that has arisen from an experiment, or something you have told them, or some other trigger. At times, the discussion may only last a short time before returning the class to your original activity. At other times, these discussions may sweep you along and into new, exciting and fruitful fields, commandeering the rest of your science time. If you judge that useful work is being done, go with the flow.

You – the teacher – are, after all, the most vital link in good education.

References

Adey, PS, Shayer, M, & Yates, C 2001, *Thinking science: The curriculum materials of the CASE project*, 3rd edn, Nelson Thornes, London.

Blackrose, MS 2011, *Myth and science: A goanna story*, viewed 13 June 2011, <http://schatzblackrose.posterous.com/myth-and-science-a-goanna-story>.

British Broadcasting Corporation (BBC) 1999, *Walking with dinosaurs*, television documentary mini-series, BBC, London.

Brown, F 2001, 'The weapon', in B Yalow (ed.), *From these ashes: The complete short SF of Fredric Brown*, The NESFA Press, Framingham, MA.

Bruner, J 1986, *Actual minds, possible worlds*, Harvard University Press, Cambridge, MA.

Cam, P 1995, *Thinking together: Philosophical inquiry for the classroom*, Primary English Teaching Association and Hale & Iremonger, Sydney.

Cam, P 2006, *Twenty thinking tools: Collaborative inquiry for the classroom*, ACER Press, Melbourne.

Clarke, AC 2000, *Profiles of the future: An enquiry into the limits of the possible*, Millennium edition, Indigo, London.

Collis, KF, Jones, BL, Sprod, TJ, Watson, JM, & Fraser, SP 1998, 'Mapping development in students' understanding of vision using a cognitive structural model', *International Journal of Science Education*, vol. 20, no.1, pp. 45–66.

Dillon, JT 1994, *Using discussion in classrooms*, Open University Press, Buckingham, PA.

Donaldson, M 1978, *Children's minds*, Fontana, London.

Driver, R, & Oldham, V 1986, 'A constructivist approach to curriculum development in science', *Studies in Science Education*, vol. 13, pp. 105–22.

Egan, K 1986, *Teaching as storytelling*, University of Chicago Press, Chicago.

Ennis, RH 1987, 'A taxonomy of critical thinking dispositions and abilities', in JB Baron and RJ Sternberg (eds), *Teaching thinking skills: Theory and practice* (pp. 9–26), Freeman, New York.

Forman, EA, & Cazden, CB 1985, 'Exploring Vygotskian perspectives in education: The cognitive value of peer interaction', in JV Wertsch (ed.), *Culture, communication and cognition: Vygotskian perspectives*, Cambridge University Press, Cambridge, pp. 323–47.

Hennessy, S 1993, 'Situated cognition and cognitive apprenticeship: Implications for classroom learning', *Studies in Science Education*, vol. 22, pp. 1–41.

Howe, AC 1996, 'Development of science concepts in a Vygotskian framework', *Science Education*, vol. 80, no. 1, pp. 35–51.

Huxley, TH, 1854, 'On the educational value of the natural history sciences', in TH Huxley, *Collected essays*, vol. 3, *Science and education*, viewed 4 July 2011, <http://aleph0.clarku.edu/huxley/CE3/EdVal.html>.

Jones, BL, Sprod, T, Collis, KF, & Watson, JM 1997, 'Singaporean and Australian students' understanding of vision', *Asia Pacific Journal of Education*, vol. 17, no. 2, pp. 85–101.

Jungk, R 1958, *Brighter than a thousand suns: A personal history of the atomic scientists*, Harcourt Brace, New York.

Kant, I 1998, *Groundwork of the metaphysics of morals,* trans. MJ Gregor, Cambridge University Press, Cambridge.

Lederman, NG, & Lederman, JS 2004, 'The nature of science and scientific inquiry', in G Venville & V Dawson (eds), *The art of teaching science*, Allen & Unwin, Sydney.

Lesser, LI, Ebbeling, CB, Goozner, M, Wypij, D, & Ludwig, DS 2007, 'Relationship between funding source and conclusion among nutrition-related scientific articles', *PLoS Medicine*, vol. 4, no. 1, article e5. doi:10.1371/journal.pmed.0040005

Lipman, M, Sharp AM, & Oscanyan, FS 1980, *Philosophy in the classroom*, Temple University Press, Philadelphia.

National Research Council 1997, *Science teaching reconsidered*, National Academy Press, Washington, DC, p. 16.

Osborne, JF, 1996, 'Beyond constructivism', *Science Education*, vol. 80, no.1, pp. 53–82.

Osborne, JF, Ratcliffe, M, Collins, S, Millar, R, & Duschl, R 2003, 'What "ideas-about-science" should be taught in school science? A Delphi Study of the "Expert" Community', *Journal of Research in Science Teaching,* vol. 40, no. 7, pp. 692–720.

Pfungst, O 1911, *Clever Hans (The horse of Mr. von Osten): A contribution to experimental animal and human psychology,* trans. CL Rahn, Henry Holt, New York.

Popper, K 1959, *The logic of scientific discovery,* Basic Books, New York.

Pratchett, T 1985, *The colour of magic,* Corgi Books, London.

Rees, WE 1992, 'Ecological footprints and appropriated carrying capacity: What urban economics leaves out', *Environment and Urbanisation,* vol. 4, no. 2, pp. 121–30.

Regan, T 1985, 'The case for animal rights' in P Singer (ed.), *In defense of animals,* Basil Blackwell, New York, pp. 13–26.

Rising, K, Bacchetti, P, & Bero, L 2008, 'Reporting bias in drug trials submitted to the Food and Drug Administration: Review of publication and presentation, *PLoS Medicine,* vol. 5, no. 11, article e217. doi:10.1371/journal.pmed.0050217

Rowe, MB 1972, *Wait-time and rewards as instructional variables: Their influence on language, logic, and fate control.* Paper presented at the National Association for Research in Science Teaching, Chicago, IL, viewed 4 July 2011, <http://eric.ed.gov:80/ERICWebPortal/search/detailmini.jsp?_nfpb=true&_&ERICExtSearch_SearchValue_0=ED061103&ERICExtSearch_SearchType_0=no&accno=ED061103>.

Rowling, JK 1997, *Harry Potter and the philosopher's stone,* Bloomsbury, London.

Rutherford, FJ, & Ahlgren, A 1991, *Science for all Americans,* Oxford University Press, New York.

Sinclair, JM, & Coulthard, RM 1975, *Towards an analysis of discourse,* Oxford University Press, Oxford.

Singer, P 1975, *Animal liberation: A new ethics for our treatment of animals,* Random House, New York.

Solomon, J 1993, *Teaching science, technology, and society,* Open University Press, Buckingham, PA.

Solomon, J 1994, 'The rise and fall of constructivism', *Studies in Science Education*, vol. 23, pp. 1–19.

Splitter, L & Sharp, AM 1995, *Teaching for better thinking: The classroom community of inquiry*, ACER Press, Melbourne.

Sprod, T 1994, 'Developing higher order thinking through whole class discussion in a science classroom', MSc thesis, Department of Educational Studies, University of Oxford.

Sprod, T 1997a, 'Improving scientific reasoning through Philosophy for Children: An empirical study', *Thinking: The Journal of Philosophy for Children*, vol. 13, no. 2, pp. 75–80.

Sprod, T 1997b, '"Nobody really knows": The structure and analysis of social constructivist whole class discussions', *International Journal of Science Education*, vol. 19, no. 8, pp. 911–24.

Sprod, T 1998, '"I can change your opinion on that": Social constructivist whole class discussions and their effect on scientific reasoning', *Research in Science Education*, vol. 28, no. 44, pp. 463–80.

Sprod, T, & Jones, BL 1997, '"The sun can't bounce off a bird": Young children and their understanding of vision', *Australian Journal of Early Childhood*, vol. 22, no. 1, pp. 29–33.

Srinivasan, UT, Carey, SP, Hallstein, E, Higgins, PT, Kerr, AC, Koteen LE, Smith, AB, Watson, R, Harte, J, & Norgaard, RB 2008, 'The debt of nations and the distribution of ecological impacts from human activities', *Proceedings of the National Academy of Sciences*, vol. 105, no. 5, pp. 1768–73.

Tytler, R 2007, 'Re-imagining science education: Engaging students in science for Australia's future', *Australian Education Review*, no. 51.

Vygotsky, LS 1962, *Thought and language*, MIT Press, Cambridge, MA.

White, RT, & Gunstone, RF 1992, *Probing understanding*, Falmer Press, London.

Zimmer, C 2011, 'It's science, but not necessarily right', *New York Times*, 25 June, 2011. Viewed 5 July 2011, <www.nytimes.com/2011/06/26/opinion/sunday/26ideas.html> on 5 July 2011>.

Further reading

Gardner, S 1995, 'Inquiry is no mere conversation', *Critical & Creative Thinking*, vol. 3, no. 2, pp. 38–49.

Splitter, L & Sprod, T 1998, *Places for thinking*, ACER Press, Melbourne.

Sprod, T 1993, *Books into ideas*, Hawker Brownlow Education, Cheltenham, VIC.

Sprod, T 2001, *Philosophical discussion in moral education: The community of ethical inquiry*, Routledge, London.

Tizard, B & Hughes, M 1984, *Young children learning: Talking and thinking at home and school*, Fontana, London.

Topping, KJ & Trickey, S 2007a, 'Collaborative philosophical enquiry for school children: Cognitive effects at 10–12 years', *British Journal of Educational Psychology*, vol. 77, no. 2, pp. 271–278.

Topping, KJ & Trickey, S 2007b, 'Collaborative philosophical enquiry for school children: Cognitive gains at 2-year follow-up', *British Journal of Educational Psychology*, vol. 77, no. 4, pp. 787–796.